PALM TREES
at the
NORTH POLE

First published in Canada, the U.S., and the U.K. by Greystone Books in 2021
Originally published in Dutch in 2018 as *Palmen op de Noordpool*
by Uitgeverij J.H. Gottmer/H.J.W. Becht bv
Text copyright © 2018 by Marc ter Horst
Illustrations copyright © 2018 by Wendy Panders
English translation copyright © 2021 by Laura Watkinson

21 22 23 24 25   5 4 3 2 1

Greystone Kids / Greystone Books Ltd.
greystonebooks.com

Cataloguing data available from Library and Archives Canada
ISBN 978-1-77164-682-6 (cloth)
ISBN 978 1 77164 683 3 (epub)

Editing by Linda Pruessen
Proofreading by Elizabeth McLean
Cover design by Sara Gillingham Studio
English text design by Fiona Siu
Printed in Singapore by COS Printers Pte Ltd

Greystone Books gratefully acknowledges the Musqueam, Squamish, and Tsleil-Waututh peoples on whose land our office is located.

This publication has been made possible with financial support from the Dutch Foundation for Literature.

Greystone Books thanks the Canada Council for the Arts, the British Columbia Arts Council, the Province of British Columbia through the Book Publishing Tax Credit, and the Government of Canada for supporting our publishing activities.

Canadä

Nederlands
letterenfonds
dutch foundation
for literature

PALM TREES
at the
NORTH POLE

The Hot Truth About
Climate Change

Written by
**MARC
ter HORST**

Illustrated by
**WENDY
PANDERS**

Translated by
LAURA WATKINSON

GREYSTONE KIDS

GREYSTONE BOOKS • VANCOUVER/BERKELEY

NORTH POLE

GREENLAND

PACIFIC
OCEAN

Shishmaref

Alaska

CANADA

NORTH
AMERICA

Vancouver
Seattle

UNITED
STATES

Toronto

New York

Los Angeles

California

MEXICO

Gulf of
Mexico

Miami

ATLANTIC
OCEAN

HAWAII

COSTA RICA

Amazon

SOUTH
AMERICA

BRAZIL

Rio de Janeir

BOLIVIA

CHILE

ANTARCTICA

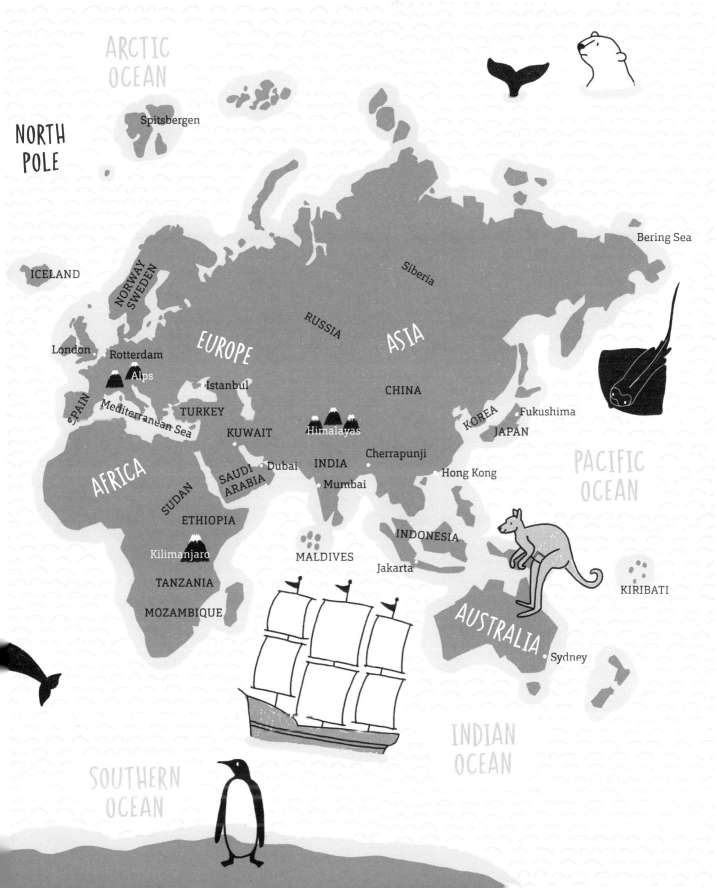

ARCTIC OCEAN

NORTH POLE

Spitsbergen

Bering Sea

ICELAND

NORWAY
SWEDEN

Siberia

EUROPE

RUSSIA

ASIA

London

Rotterdam

Alps

CHINA

KOREA

Fukushima

Istanbul

JAPAN

SPAIN

Mediterranean Sea

TURKEY

KUWAIT

Himalayas

Cherrapunji

PACIFIC OCEAN

Dubai

INDIA

AFRICA

SAUDI
ARABIA

Mumbai

Hong Kong

SUDAN

ETHIOPIA

MALDIVES

INDONESIA

Kilimanjaro

Jakarta

KIRIBATI

TANZANIA

MOZAMBIQUE

AUSTRALIA

Sydney

INDIAN OCEAN

SOUTHERN OCEAN

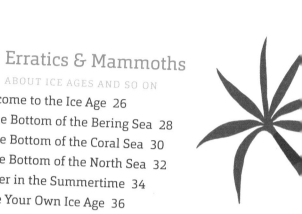

Once upon a time, there were palm trees at the North Pole. Can you picture that? The most tropical of trees in a place where now there is only snow and ice. In the future, they might reappear. Because the climate is constantly changing. During the ice ages, it was much colder than it is now. In the days of the dinosaurs, it was much warmer.

However, in recent years, the climate has been changing pretty quickly. That's why so many people are talking about climate change. It's a complicated story though, involving bits of physics, chemistry, geology, biology, meteorology, and other sciences. How can amateurs like you and me ever hope to understand? Because of course we want to know what's going on with the polar bears, the hurricanes, and all the fires and flooding.

That's why I've spent a few years collecting information from all over the place—from the internet, newspapers, television, books, and from people who know lots about the subject. I've put it all together for you, and for me, in a way that should make sense, at least most of the time. But if there's something you don't understand, it's not a big deal. Keep going and you'll soon get it.

8
·
9

You're going to see that the big story of climate change is about much more than polar bears and exhaust gases. That's why it takes a bit for them to come into the story. First we need to talk about volcanoes, mammoths, and shivering scientists. Then you can read all about climate change today. What's going to change? Who will be affected? Where? Why? When? How? Is it real? And will you still be able to take a hot shower every day?

1 · Snowballs & Volcanoes

In which you will read… that the history of the Earth has had a lot of ups and downs • where the first rain came from • how the Earth changed into a snowball from top to bottom • what sort of scary critters crept and crawled among the first plants • why the dinosaurs died out • how a few giant farts from the sea caused a heat wave.

In short: about the early history of the climate.

The Old, Old Earth

You might think your mom and dad are old. That the pyramids are ancient. Or that the dinosaurs you can see at the natural history museum are the oldest thing ever. But all of those are nothing compared to the age of the Earth. Our planet is already more than 4.5 billion years old. That's about ten times as old as the first trilobites that swam in the oceans. A hundred times as old as the Himalayas. More than a thousand times as old as Lucy, one of the first humanoids. Ten thousand times as old as the saber-toothed tigers in their heyday. A hundred thousand times as old as the first rock drawings that humans made. A million times as old as the Egyptian pyramids. Nearly ten million times as old as the *Mona Lisa*. And around a hundred million times as old as your mom and dad. Now that's old.

I bet your mom and dad have changed quite a bit over the years. They probably look way different now than they do in their childhood photographs. The pyramids have changed a lot over the course of time too. They've worn down to the point where there is almost nothing left of some of them. The trilobites died out long ago. And so did the saber-toothed tiger.

In the same way, the Earth is no longer what it once was. Over many millions of years, it has continued to change and evolve. A hundred million years ago, America and Europe were attached to each other. At that time, Australia was not yet an island—but India was. Mountain ranges have come and gone. The Earth was once entirely covered with lava and once completely under snow and ice. The water in the oceans was sometimes higher and sometimes much lower than it is now.

The layer of air around the Earth has not remained the same either. There was a time when there was much more oxygen in the air than there is now, but also a time when there was no oxygen in the air at all. So it's good to be aware that the Earth is constantly changing. This is true for the land, for the water, and for the air—and so it's true for the climate too.

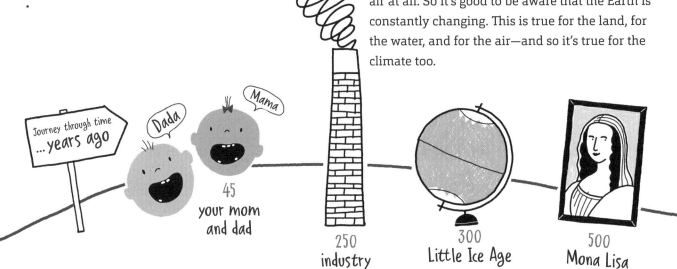

Journey through time ...years ago

Dada

Mama

45
your mom
and dad

250
industry

300
Little Ice Age

500
Mona Lisa

66 million
dinosaurs died out

55 million
palm trees at the
North Pole

45 million
Himalayas

Lucy
3.2 million

300 million
coal

BIRTH OF
EARTH

4,500 million
years ago

O2   CO2

3,500 million
photosynthesis

2.5 million
ice ages begin

450 million
plants on land
trilobites

700 million
snowball Earth

450.000
saber-toothed tiger

4,500
pyramids

10,000
end of last ice age

45,000
rock drawing

The First Two Billion Years

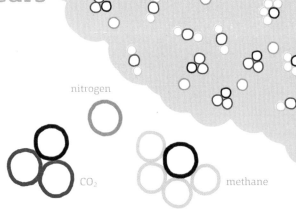

When the Earth had just recently come into existence, it was really, really hot. There weren't any thermometers or weather forecasters around to measure just how hot, but it got up to around 2,000 degrees Celsius. It was so hot that the outer layer of the Earth was completely melted. Our planet was one big ball of lava.

A thin layer of air developed around the Earth: the atmosphere. The air did not yet contain any oxygen, the wonderful gas that we breathe in about 1,000 times an hour. But it did have nitrogen, and methane and carbon dioxide. That last one is a bit of a mouthful and it gets mentioned a lot, so we've shortened it to CO_2, like the scientists do. It's pronounced "see oh two."

Methane and CO_2 are very good at holding on to heat. That's why it was so hot on Earth. The atmosphere worked like a greenhouse, one of those glass buildings where plants and vegetables are grown. The glass lets in the sunlight and keeps the heat for a very long time. So this "greenhouse effect" makes the planet nice and warm. But it is possible to have too much of a good thing.

In the early years of our planet, it was like hell on Earth: a temperature of thousands of degrees, volcanoes erupting all over the place, a sea of stinking lava, and air that was too toxic to breathe. But there was worse to come. A bombardment of meteorites hit the Earth. For hundreds of millions of years, huge rocks and blocks of ice fell from space onto our planet. The ice melted and evaporated. As a result, the air came to contain more and more water vapor—water in the form of gas. You can't see it, but it's all around you even now.

The water cooled the surface of the Earth a lot, taking it down to around 200 degrees. In many places, the lava began to harden. And hard lava is—yes, that's right—stone. That's how the crust we live on was formed. The ice of the meteorites was still melting, but it didn't all evaporate. Liquid water filled the oceans. And the water vapor became the first rain.

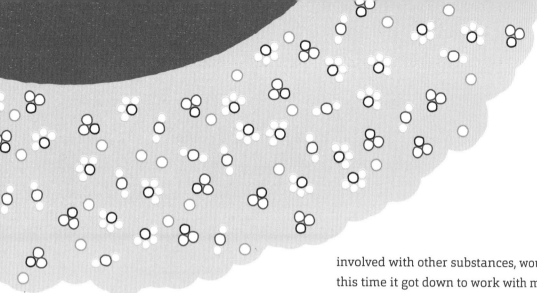

So wasn't there any oxygen on Earth at all? Yes, there was oxygen, but it was trapped in water and stone. You see, oxygen is pretty pushy stuff. It wants to connect with everything. And when it connects with hydrogen, it forms water. Together with iron and water, it creates rust. Combined with methane, it makes water and CO_2.

Luckily, at a certain point, bacteria developed that turn CO_2 into oxygen. This process is known as photosynthesis. Together with sunlight and water, the bacteria broke the CO_2 into pieces, creating carbon (C) and oxygen (O_2). The bacteria built their tiny little bodies out of the carbon. And the oxygen, of course, immediately went off to make more connections with iron and other metals. But after a while the metals had had enough. There was no room for more oxygen

The only place for the oxygen to go was into the air. High up in the air, the oxygen formed an important protective layer against the sun's ultraviolet rays: the ozone layer. But oxygen wouldn't be oxygen if it didn't start getting

involved with other substances, would it? And this time it got down to work with methane. There was plenty of methane in the atmosphere. When oxygen encounters methane, it turns it into CO_2. As a greenhouse gas, that's annoying, but it's not as bad as methane.

So, the oxygen made CO_2 out of methane, and the bacteria made oxygen out of CO_2. This gradually made the atmosphere less... greenhousy.

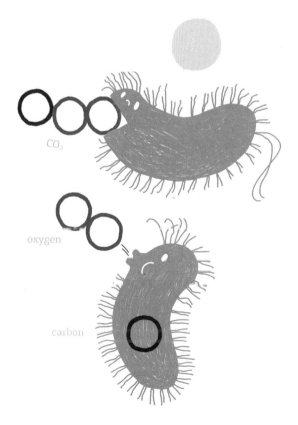

CO_2

oxygen

carbon

The Snowball Effect

The biggest snowball in the world formed around 700 million years ago. It was as big as the world, because it *was* the world! The average temperature on Earth had dropped to 45 degrees Celsius below zero. For millions of years, the world was covered with a layer of ice that was more than a kilometer thick. There was no need to be scared of falling through it, but then there weren't any people around yet who might want to go skating.

The only life that existed was our teeny tiny little ancient ancestors: the bacteria who were busily working away to turn CO_2 into oxygen. By doing this, they caused a kind of reverse greenhouse effect. More and more oxygen entered the air, and less and less CO_2. This made the Earth colder and colder.

They were causing problems for themselves too though, because it's not easy to survive on a frozen planet. If you're unlucky, you could find yourself and your entire bacteria family shivering away around a deep-sea volcano, just waiting for the world to thaw.

But how did that snowball Earth develop? It obviously began with a huge cooling-off period. That might well have been the work of the bacteria, but scientists have also considered other causes: maybe a weak moment for the sun, a bump in the Earth's path, or the eruption of a super-volcano darkening the skies with huge amounts of dust. Whatever the case, it got colder on Earth. The ice at both poles grew bigger.

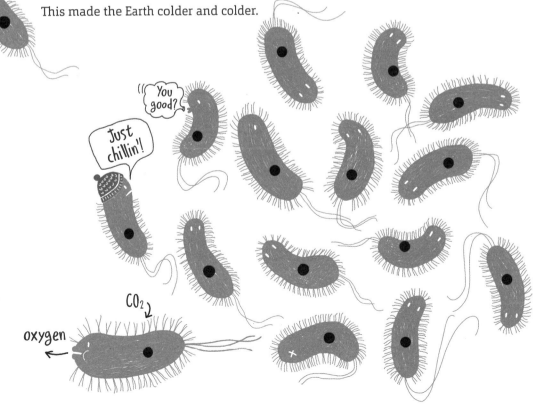

That ice was, of course, white, and so it reflected the sun much better than the ground or the water. As a result, lots of the heat vanished back into space, and it became even colder on Earth. The ice grew and grew and reflected even more sunlight. The white ice worked as a climate amplifier: the coldness made sure that it became colder and colder.

All around the world, the seas froze over. Even at the equator, there was a thick layer of ice and snow. (Although some scientists believe that there was never anything more than a bit of mushy wet snow in that region, and that it frequently thawed.)

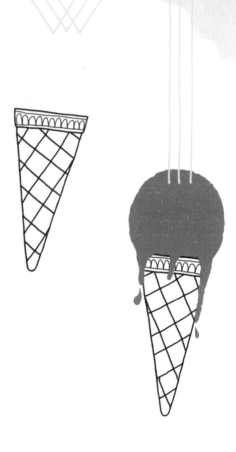

For millions of years, the Earth drifted through the universe as a white world of ice. Most species of bacteria died out. A few kinds were able to survive, but only the ones that lived near volcanoes. Those volcanoes must have also caused the ice to thaw again. The interior of the Earth was still a bubbling mass of hot rock. It crackled and hissed away beneath the ice. Eventually, the lava found ways out in more and more places. It wasn't the heat that made the ice thaw though. It was the greenhouse gases CO_2 and methane, which the volcanoes blew into the air. These are gases that hold on to heat. This made it more difficult for the sunlight that was reflected off the ice to disappear back into space. The ice melted in lots of different places. White was replaced by darker colors that were better at holding on to the heat. As a result, the Earth became warmer and warmer. Within no time, the snowball had melted.

Long Live Carbon

Let's go back 500 million years in time. The Earth is celebrating its four billionth birthday, and the trilobites have been invited to the party. It has warmed up quite a lot since the Earth was a snowball. All kinds of new forms of life are developing in the sea: strange creatures with eyes on stalks, wacky feelers, funny little trunks, mean-looking spikes, and complicated tentacles. But above water, there is absolutely nothing going on. Just rocks and lava. There is not a living creature to be seen anywhere, not even a tiny clump of moss.

But then, very cautiously, the first plants start heading out onto the land. The air is still packed with CO_2, but that's handy: plants need CO_2 to grow. Just like bacteria, they use sunlight and water to make carbohydrates out of CO_2. And then they make leaves, twigs, branches, and fruit out of the carbohydrates. The oxygen that is left over disappears back into the air.

Using this method, the plants slowly conquer the world, popping up all over the place and growing like crazy. This means that less and less CO_2 goes into the air—and more and more oxygen. And that makes the world above water suitable for animals too. There are no dinosaurs or mammals yet, but there are giant insects and other big scary critters. How would you like to meet spiders as big as a meter across, dragonflies with wings of half a meter, and centipedes that are longer than people?

Animals need carbohydrates to grow and as a source of energy. They eat plants to get their dose of carbohydrates. They breathe oxygen so that they can burn the food—not on a fire but inside their bodies, just like you. During this burning process, CO_2 is released. The animals breathe it out. And the plants put that CO_2 to good use.

This means that carbon is always moving from place to place. It is in the air, in a plant, in the ground, or in an animal. It mixes with all kinds of other little particles. Together with oxygen, it forms CO_2. With hydrogen, it forms methane. And with oxygen and hydrogen, it makes carbohydrates. No living creature can do without it. If you divide your weight by five, you'll find out how many kilograms of carbon are inside you.

When people, animals, and plants die, the carbon is released into the air again. This happens

because they rot and decay: bacteria and molds break everything down. Try leaving an apple or a sandwich on a plate for weeks. You'll see—and smell!—the change for yourself. Eventually, what is left of the carbohydrates is carbon and oxygen: CO_2. This rotting process requires lots of oxygen though. If there isn't much around, the bacteria are unable to make any CO_2. So they turn the carbon into methane instead, which is made up of carbon and hydrogen.

But if there is no oxygen around, bacteria and molds can't get much done. Consider, for example, what happens when a plant falls into the water. Back in the days of the big scary critters, there was a high chance of that happening, as lots of plants and trees grew in swamps. In a swamp, no oxygen can get to the dead remains of the plant. So the plant doesn't rot, and the carbon disappears deep into the ground.

For hundreds of millions of years, trees and plants disappeared into swamps. All their lives, they had taken CO_2 out of the air, and now they took it with

them under the ground. So CO_2 slowly disappeared from the air, and less CO_2 means less heat. Ice caps grew again at the North Pole and the South Pole. But this time the planet did not turn into a snowball Earth. The cold stayed near the poles. Between the poles, it was a good deal warmer. Just like now, there were lots of different climates on Earth.

O_2 = oxygen

CO_2

C

dead animals and plants

C = carbon

What Finished Off the Dinosaurs?

Around 230 million years ago, the era of the dinosaurs began. In all kinds of shapes and sizes, they stomped and scampered and flew across the Earth—until 66 million years ago, when a big meteorite fell from the sky. They had survived for almost 165 million years, but that meteorite killed off most of them. What does this have to do with the climate? More than you might think.

One hundred and sixty-five million years is a long period of time. At the beginning, all the continents were attached to one another. Together, they formed one massive continent that we now call Pangaea. In most places, it was warm, warmer than it is now. But there were big differences in climate between the coastal areas and the land in the middle.

At the edges of Pangaea, it was damp. That was because these areas bordered on the oceans, where the rain came from. The land in the middle of the continent was much drier. It had a desert climate. The rain hardly ever came that far. It was like the middle of Australia is now. Also, in the center, it was ice cold at night and in the winter, but extremely hot in the daytime and the summer. Closer to the sea, these differences weren't as extreme. That's because water cools down and warms up more slowly than land. And the temperature of the sea has a lot of influence on coastal regions. You can see this in cities like Seattle or Vancouver. Their position by the sea means that they often have kind of patchy winters, while it's absolutely freezing in Chicago, Calgary, and Toronto.

But Pangaea did not remain whole. This enormous region broke apart into different pieces. Eventually the continents drifted away from one another to form the world map that we know today. That

meant there were lots more regions that bordered the sea. The climate became wetter, and differences in temperature grew smaller and smaller. Even at the North Pole, it was hotter than it is now in Canada or Great Britain. This meant that the dinosaurs were able to conquer the whole world, from the North Pole to the South Pole and everything in between. And they managed to do it all without fur coats.

But, as you know, 66 million years ago, the dinosaurs died out. Most scientists think this was because of an enormous rock from space that fell to Earth. In Mexico, you can find the Chicxulub crater, which is 150 kilometers in diameter—bigger than New Jersey. It must have been formed by a meteorite with a diameter of at least 10 kilometers. The dinosaurs didn't die because that huge rock fell on their heads, though (well, except for a few dinosaurs who happened to be in the wrong place at the wrong time). But maybe they were the lucky ones. At least they didn't have to suffer the terrible consequences of the impact.

Because you could certainly say that the meteorite kicked up a whole lot of dust. For years, the sun was darkened. This caused problems for plants and algae. They need sunlight to survive. A lot of plants died, and so the plant-eating dinosaurs died as well. And when the meat-eating dinosaurs had finished off the last plant-eating dinosaur, there was not much left for them to eat either. With rumbling stomachs, the last of the dinosaurs met their sad and sorry end.

The impact of the meteorite most likely caused big forest fires too. Those fires killed off many trees, releasing a lot of CO_2 into the air. You already know what that means: extra greenhouse gases and, therefore, extra heat. That wouldn't have made it any easier for the weakened dinosaurs to survive.

There was also an unstoppable volcanic eruption in India at the time. The lava went on bubbling out for millions of years—until there was a layer two kilometers thick covering an area roughly the size of Texas. The volcano pumped a huge load of CO_2 and dust into the air. The dust darkened the sun, which at first made it colder for a few years, and the plants died. But then later it became warmer, because of the CO_2 from the volcano and the dead plants.

So you can see that there are lots of things that have an influence on the climate. A changing map of the world can make it wetter or drier. Meteorites, forest fires, and volcanoes put extra CO_2 and extra dust in the air. The CO_2 warms the Earth. The dust cools the Earth because the sunlight is unable to get through. But it also causes plants to die, and so extra CO_2 is released again.

The last of the dinosaurs got to see all of that for themselves. They were confronted with major natural disasters. All those disasters had an impact on the climate at the time. And the climate had a disastrous effect on the dinosaurs.

Farts from the Sea

In our time, the North Pole and Antarctica (the South Pole) are both bare, dry, icy regions without much life. However, 55 million years ago, these areas were covered with trees. It was 25 degrees Celsius, and even during the dark polar nights the temperature did not go below zero. Palm trees grew at the North Pole, trees that naturally grow only in warm climates. So, back then, there was no sign of ice at the poles. Polar bears and arctic hares had not yet put in an appearance. Instead, what lived at the North Pole was the ancestors of crocodiles and hippos.

Within the space of 20,000 years, it had become at least five degrees hotter, all over the world. According to geologists and climatologists, this is an incredible change—and it happened super fast. This rise in temperature was due to the sudden increase of CO_2 in the air. This may have been because of volcanic eruptions, but they don't know that for certain. The heat wave was probably made even worse by giant farts from the sea.

Those farts were mainly made up of methane gas that had been lying safely at the bottom of the oceans for millions of years. The methane was produced by the decaying remains of animals and plants. You know how it works: if there's no oxygen around, the bacteria like to make things into methane instead. Because of the

cold at the bottom of the ocean, the methane was more or less frozen down there. Until it became warmer, that is. Then the methane was released, but it couldn't go anywhere. So the pressure became greater and greater. You probably know the feeling. Finally, it was impossible to keep it in. With huge explosions, the methane escaped from the ocean floor, rising up in enormous bubbles and bursting out of the sea. Boom—into the atmosphere. Together with the CO_2, the methane ensured that Earth remained a greenhouse for many more years. Since then, it has never been that hot on Earth again.

Around 35 million years ago, Australia and South America broke away from Antarctica. As a result, the cold water by the South Pole began flowing around. Warmer water could no longer reach Antarctica, and so this part of the world rapidly cooled down. The trees disappeared. The ice cap formed. The cold water became even colder and cooled the rest of the oceans too. The planet was ready for the ice ages.

2 · Erratics & Mammoths

In which you will read... why not all ice ages are the same • how Native Americans and First Nations peoples came to America • how Australia's big coral reef developed • what the people at the bottom of the North Sea used to eat • where they celebrate Christmas in bikinis • what the recipe for a perfect ice age is • that it's not the sunspots' fault.

In short: about ice ages and so on.

Welcome to the Ice Age

Now I need to tell you something that not a lot of people know. Something that might not make you happy—or maybe it will. It might send shivers down your spine. Would you like me just to tell you? Actually… actually… actually we're in the middle of an ice age right now. No, really. It's true! You and me and all the people in the world are slap bang in the middle of an ice age—now and yesterday and all our lives. It is, of course, a somewhat warmer period within that ice age, but officially it's an ice age. Because geologists describe a time as an ice age if there are large ice caps to be found on land somewhere on the Earth. Geologists are people who study the Earth—so they should know. And they're right. Just take a look at Antarctica and Greenland. The ice there is a couple of kilometers thick on average, and in some places thicker than the height of Pikes Peak. If those aren't big ice caps, then I don't know what is. They've been there for 2.5 million years. So all that time we've been living in an ice age. The same ice age as the mammoths and the saber-toothed tigers. But they lived in a colder phase of this ice age, the kind of period that ordinary people like you and me call an ice age. That's what lots of books and websites will tell you too, by the way, and that's what you're used to, unless you happen to be a geologist.

So we have a little problem. You can't really say that there were ice ages in the ice age. So what should we do? Should we join in with the geologists and say that it's been an ice age for 2.5 million years? Or do we just call the extra-cold periods ice ages, as we're used to doing? That might make it easier for our brains to handle. Otherwise they'll have to turn everything upside down and shift the mammoths and the bearskins from one brain cell to another. That seems like a lot of trouble. So let's agree that in this book an ice age is only an ice age if it's a lot colder than it is now.

so hot

In the past 2.5 million years, there have been around 25 ice ages like that, extra-cold periods when the ice didn't stay at the North and South Poles, but grew more and more, so that even in the summertime it reached as far as Canada, Sweden, and central Russia. As the ice expanded, it pushed sand, clay, and rocks in front of it, flattening hills and forests. At the tips of these expanses of ice, new hills grew in the landscape, hills that we now think are perfectly ordinary. Sometimes the ice came as far south as the Canadian border. Sometimes farther and sometimes not as far. But the consequences of every ice age were huge.

During an ice age, more snow falls than rain. All the snow that falls on the land and on the ice stays on the ground and holds on to the water. That means that much less water flows back into the seas, but water still continues to evaporate. As a result, the level of the water in the seas goes down, and people and animals can walk across the bottom of the sea. Sounds like fun!

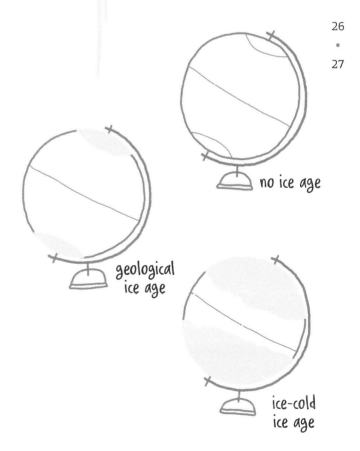

no ice age

geological
ice age

ice-cold
ice age

At the Bottom of the Bering Sea

If you look closely, you may be able to see it. Some of the indigenous peoples of America—the Native Americans and First Nations—look a little Asian. They have dark, straight hair, and their eyes and skin color are often similar to those of people from China, for instance. This is not just a coincidence—and it has something to do with the ice age.

The first human beings originated in Africa. All modern people are descended from them. More and more people came along, so some families began to move away. First they went to Europe and Asia. It took tens of thousands of years for anyone to reach the extreme east of Asia. Very slowly, from parent to child, the appearance of human beings changed. They developed lighter skins. That was handy in areas farther from the equator, where the sun didn't rise as high, because a lighter skin helps your body to make enough vitamin D, even with only a little sunlight.

Asia and America are separated by the Bering Sea. Anyone who wants to cross the sea has to sail 80 kilometers. Twenty thousand years ago, there was no need to do that—because, back then, Asia and America were attached to each other. Because of the ice age, lots of water was stored in ice caps. So much water, in fact, that the sea level all over the entire world was 120 meters lower. The people who arrived in America lived for thousands of years on what is now the bottom of the sea. Let's hope they made a fire or two, because it was really, really cold. When the ice began to melt, some groups moved on and populated the north of North America—the

area we now know as Canada. Others went south, to what is now the United States. They settled in different areas, but they were the first people to call the North American continent home.

When these human beings came to America, they encountered all kinds of big animals. Animals like the giant beaver, the cave lion, the saber-toothed tiger, the dire wolf, the mammoth, and the *Megatherium*, a ground sloth that was the size of an elephant. Most of these giant animals had been living there for millions of years. They'd never seen a human being before. A few thousand years later, all the giant animals in North and South America were extinct. Was that because humans hunted them? That's certainly what the evidence suggests.

At the Bottom of the Coral Sea

The biggest coral reef in the world is in the Coral Sea off the northeast coast of Australia. This reef is made entirely of coral organisms, and it is called the Great Barrier Reef. In total, the reef is about 2,600 kilometers long. It is made up of 900 islands and lots and lots of reefs, all of which are just under the water surface. There are large numbers of colorful fish and other creatures swimming around in the sea there—a lot like Nemo and Dory, but with smaller eyes, not as many friends, and way more boring lives.

Climate change is a huge threat to the Great Barrier Reef. But we'll get to that later. Climate change was also responsible for the creation of the reef, as scientists have only recently discovered. The original inhabitants of the region, the Aboriginals, had known about it for a long time though.

Like the first Americans, the Aboriginals were able to make the crossing from Asia thanks to the ice age. Nowadays, you'd need something like a ferry or an airplane. But back then the water of the sea was so low that nearly all the islands of Indonesia were attached to one another. The Aboriginals could walk from Sumatra to Java and Bali. There were just a few deeper spots where they must have used boats to get all the way to Australia.

They arrived there about 50,000 years ago. The Aboriginals spread out across Australia. The Yidindji people went to live on the coast of the Coral Sea, where, at that time, there was no coral at all. They lived there for tens of thousands of years, on a large plain beside the sea. They collected shells from among the rocks, caught fish in the sea, and hunted water birds in the forests on the coast.

What's fascinating is that the Aboriginals of today still know the stories of their distant ancestors. The older people pass on the stories to their children and grandchildren in the form of a dance and a kind of song. One of these dances tells the

story of Gunyah and the sacred fish. Gunyah goes fishing with his spear. He throws the spear at a sparkle in the water. But—oh no!—it turns out to be a whiptail stingray, their sacred fish! The fish becomes angry and rises up, thrashing about and setting the sea in motion so that the water rises higher and higher.

That is how the Aboriginals tell the story of the rise in the sea level, a story that is completely in line with the latest scientific research. Well, okay, except for the bit about the angry fish. But around 14,000 years ago, the water did indeed begin to rise. It was the end of the ice age and the ice caps were melting. The plain where the Yidindji lived gradually became covered with water. The land turned into swamp, the swamp turned into sea, and the little hills turned into islands. Where there had once been a plain, there was now a warm, shallow sea. It was the perfect place for a big coral reef to grow. Because in a shallow sea, the sun can reach all the way to the bottom—and the algae in the coral need sunlight to grow. That was how, over the course of a few thousand years, the largest living construction on Earth was created: the Great Barrier Reef.

At the Bottom of the North Sea

If you stand on the beach on the coast of the Netherlands or the east coast of England, you'll find yourself looking out across the endless surface of the North Sea. All you'll be able to see on the water is a few fishing boats and maybe some cargo ships making their way to a nearby harbor. It's hard to imagine that under those ships, in the gray mass of water, millions of creatures are living their daily lives. Sharks are hunting for herring. Plaice are hiding away in the sand. The hermit crab is looking for a new house. Unseen by your eyes, countless nature films are taking place, all at once.

However, it's even more difficult to imagine what it was like here thousands of years ago. First you'll have to drain the sea. On the bottom you'll find the bones of mammoths, cave lions, hyenas, horses, and rhinoceroses. These are all animals that lived here 50,000 years ago. This part of the North Sea was once a big grassy plain. There were hills, rivers flowed, and trees and bushes grew. The world was in the middle of an ice age. Most of the water between the Netherlands and England had disappeared.

Fishing trawlers out on the North Sea regularly find these old bones in their nets. Occasionally they also find traces of human beings, such as hand axes and antlers with small decorations carved on them. Around 10,000 years ago, human beings lived as hunter-gatherers on the low-lying plain between England, the Netherlands, and Denmark, an area we now call Doggerland. They made huts out of branches, canoes from tree trunks, and arrow-heads of stone. There was plenty of food to be found in the area. With a little luck, they could have a different meal every night: Monday—venison steaks; Tuesday—mussels; Wednesday—duck leg; Thursday—elk nuggets; Friday—fish soup; Saturday—boar stew; and Sunday—otter burgers. But you and I already know that the Doggerlanders won't be able to stay there. The ice is going to melt. The North Sea is on its way!

The meltwater from the ice caps made the sea level rise—by about two meters a century. First the water channels of Doggerland filled up. The area became wetter and wetter. Deer, elk, and boars quickly got out of there. But the Doggerlanders stayed. There were enough places left where the water wasn't a problem. They did have to adapt their diet a little though. From then on, they ate water birds, otters, and fish a bit more often. But the water went on rising.

We don't know if the last Doggerlanders survived. Maybe they went to live high and dry on Dogger Bank, a ridge of hills that slowly became an island. Or maybe they retreated to the mainland. Let's hope they did. Because around 8,200 years ago, there was a landslide off the coast of Norway that caused a huge tidal wave—a real tsunami, which flooded all the coasts of the North Sea, and that would certainly have included Dogger Bank. Whatever happened, no arrowheads or other human traces have been found from after that date. So, by that point, all the inhabitants had disappeared from the bottom of the sea.

Winter in the Summertime

During the last ice age, it was four degrees colder on average than it is now. That's quite some climate change. For thousands of years, it was nonstop winter in much of the world. And around every 100,000 years, that long, long winter comes back again. In the next section, you'll find a recipe for these ice ages. But first it might be handy for you to know how our seasons work.

Why is it warm in the summer and cold in the winter? Lots of people think it's because the Earth is closer to the sun in the summer than it is in the winter. But that's complete nonsense. Because while it's summer in the Northern Hemisphere, it's winter in the Southern Hemisphere. Then, half a year later, it's the other way around: then it's winter for us and summer in Australia. So they can celebrate Christmas in Australia wearing bikinis and swim trunks on the beach.

It is true, though, that the Earth isn't always the same distance from the sun. The Earth circles the sun once a year. That circle isn't actually a circle though, but an ellipse. It's like the shape of a Hula-Hoop when you lean on it a bit. When it's

summer in the Northern Hemisphere, the Earth is actually five million kilometers *farther away* from the sun than in the winter. Half a year later, it's the other way around: it's summer in the Southern Hemisphere and the Earth is *closer* to the sun than in the southern winter. So, the distance from the sun doesn't have that much influence on the seasons.

No, seasons happen because the Earth is a little bit tilted. In our summer, the Northern Hemisphere is turned to the sun. You can tell that because the days are longer and the sun is higher. Longer days give the sun more time to warm the Earth. And when the sun is higher, its rays travel a shorter distance through the atmosphere, so more heat remains. The rays of sun are also extra strong: every piece of skin or earth receives more sun than in the winter. You can easily imitate this with a flashlight or a spotlight. Point the flashlight straight at the wall, so that you see a nice round circle of light. That's how the sun shines when it's high in the sky. Now shine the light onto the wall at an angle. The same amount of light comes out, but it's spread over a larger area. So every piece of wall gets less light and less warmth—just like the Earth in the winter.

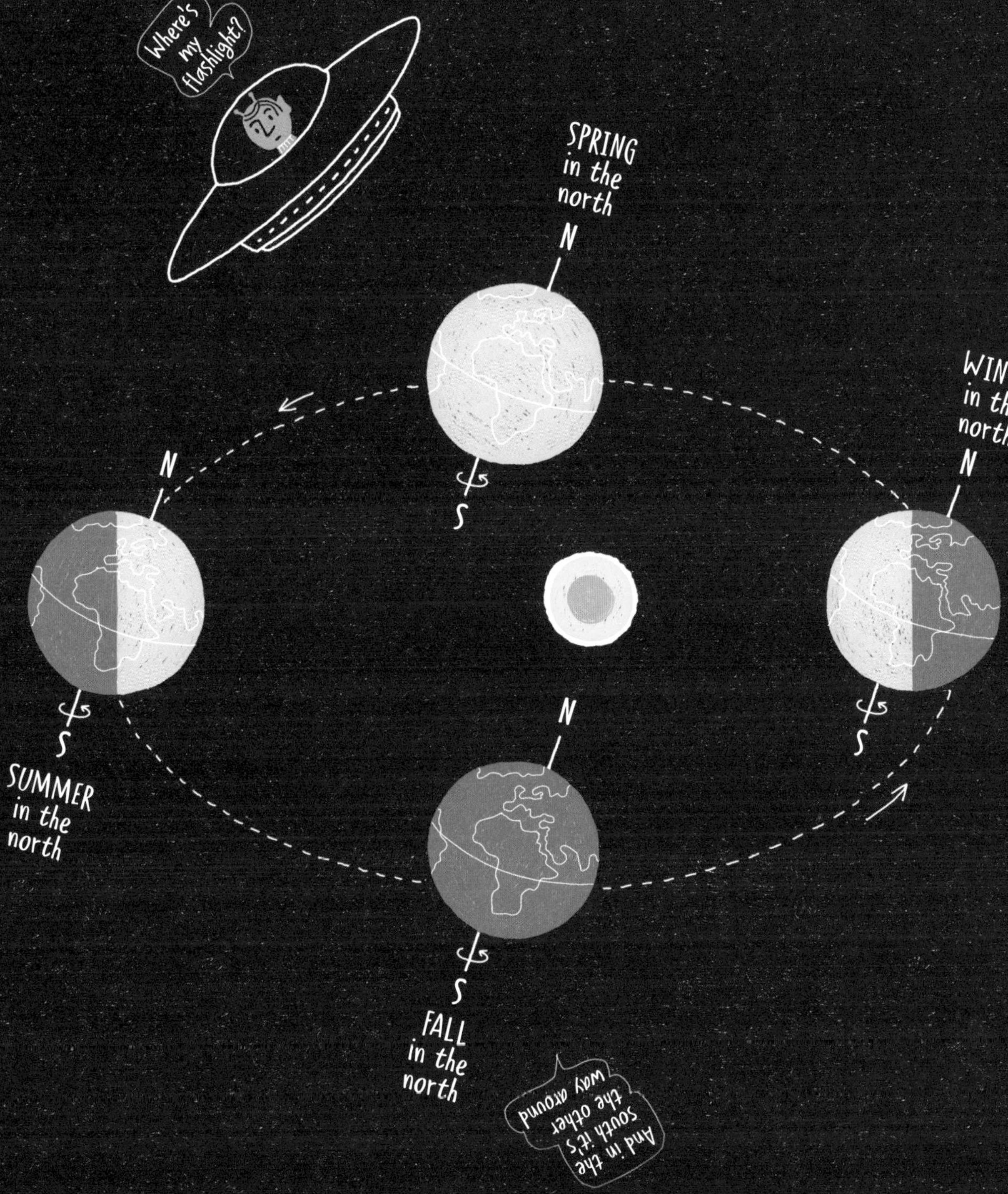

Where's my flashlight?
SPRING in the north
N
S
WINTER in the north
N
S
SUMMER in the north
N
S
FALL in the north
N
S
And in the south it's the other way around

Make Your Own Ice Age

The recipe for an ice age is mainly a question of waiting. The most important factor is that, year after year, more snow falls than melts. So how do you make that happen?

Make sure the continents are positioned well, and not all huddled together as in the age of the dinosaurs. To make an ice age, a good portion of the land has to be covered with ice. This can only happen when there's a lot of land located in cold areas—so around the poles, as is now the case with Antarctica at the South Pole and with Alaska, Canada, Greenland, Scandinavia, and Russia around the North Pole. This means that lots of snow falls not into the sea, but onto the land, where it can stick around.

Make sure that a lot of moisture goes to the poles. This is needed to make snow. For millions of years, there were no ice ages. This was probably because there was a gap between North America and South America. All that time, the fish could easily swim back and forth between the Pacific Ocean and the Atlantic Ocean. The water flowed happily between North America and South America too. But the two areas of land moved very slowly toward each other, until the connection between the two oceans was closed. No more fish could get through. The water could only pass from one ocean to the other in the far north and the far south of the globe. The currents in the ocean changed completely. This meant that more damp air went to the north, where it created more snow.

Make sure you have mild winters and cool summers in the Northern Hemisphere, where the snow is more likely to stay lying on the ground. During a mild winter, more water evaporates than in a cold winter. This evaporation is needed to

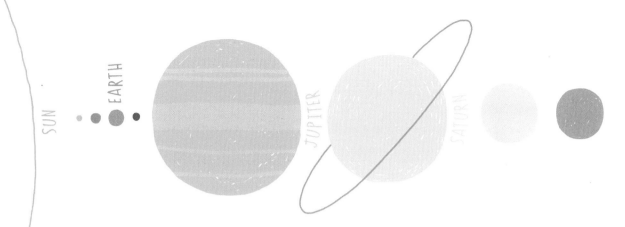

make snow. And in the cool summer, much of that snow then remains on the ground. To make the winters milder and the summers cooler, you need to use the giant planets Jupiter and Saturn. With their huge gravity, they constantly pull at the Earth. This has consequences for our orbit around the sun. Sometimes the orbit is almost round, and sometimes it's a bit more elongated. Sometimes the Earth is a little tilted, and sometimes it's a little more tilted. Sometimes in summer the north is closer to the sun, and sometimes the south. Every hundred thousand years or so, the planets are perfectly positioned to unleash an ice age. Then the path of the Earth around the sun is very elongated, the Earth is not as tilted, and the distance between the Earth and the sun is at its greatest during the northern summertime. Then the differences between the seasons are smaller than they are now. During such an ice age, the northern winters are mild enough to make lots of snow fall and the summers are cold enough to keep the snow from melting.

Got it all? Then you can calmly sit back and wait a few thousand years. Climate amplifiers will do the rest. Because the ice is growing and growing, the Earth steadily becomes a little whiter. You know what happens then: the rays of the sun are reflected back and the Earth cools off even more. This means that the layers of snow become thicker and thicker. They grow kilometers high—to an altitude where it's colder, and so the snow does not melt as quickly. Because it is colder, less water evaporates, and there is less water vapor in the air. Water vapor holds on to the heat. So, less water vapor means less heat. The cold makes plants and dead plant matter freeze. They do not have the chance to start rotting. As a result, their carbon stays trapped in the ice for the time being and they are unable to release any CO_2 into the air. The oceans also hold on to more CO_2 because it is cold. And less CO_2 means less heat.

Are you tired of your ice age? Then put Saturn and Jupiter back where they were. With warmer summers and cooler winters, the ice caps will melt by themselves. More CO_2 will be released into the air and the Earth will warm up again.

Volcanic Dust and Sunspots

The last ice age was a while ago now, and we're going to be waiting a while for the next one. Right now, the Earth is not in a favorable position for a real ice age. The planet is too tilted and the orbit around the sun is too round. For the past 15,000 years, the Earth has been thawing almost nonstop. The glaciers have just kept on melting. Water levels in the seas have risen by meters per century. Areas that were attached to each other became separated. Great Britain became an island, along with Japan, Tasmania, Sumatra, and Java. The higher temperatures and the disappearing snow meant that trees could grow again. Primeval forests were advancing all over North America, Europe, and Asia. The ice age was at an end. But even so…

A few centuries ago, it suddenly became really cold again. For this reason, the period from around the 15th to the 19th century is sometimes called the Little Ice Age. Paintings from that time feature a surprising number of wintery scenes. Crops failed, rivers froze over, and the glaciers grew bigger again. A thousand years ago, however, it was extra-warm. During that period, Europe had very good harvests. Lots of wine was cultivated, all the way to the middle of England, and peaches grew on trees in Belgium.

We're not entirely sure what caused these differences. Most scientists blame volcanoes. One thousand years ago, they were keeping calm and not blowing their tops, so there was not much dust to stop the sun's rays getting through. Six hundred years ago, however, there were a few big volcanic eruptions. The dust from the volcanoes blocked the sunlight, the Earth cooled down, and the ice grew. But there is another suspect that might be responsible for the heat of 1,000 years ago and the cold of 500 years ago: sunspots.

Sunspots are dark spots on the sun. They look like little dots, but they can actually be bigger than the Earth. These spots are dark because they are a little cooler than the rest of the sun. They come and go with a rhythm of around 11 years. When there are a lot of sunspots, the sun is extra active. This also makes the northern lights more likely, by the way—you know, those dancing green curtains of light you can sometimes see in Alaska and Canada's north.

You'd think that the activity of the sun would have an influence on the climate on Earth. That more solar activity causes warming and less results in cooling. During the Little Ice Age, there were indeed oddly low numbers of sunspots—at least if you believe the reports written by astronomers at the time. But it seems that they didn't record everything—far from it, in fact. So there's a good chance that there were just as many sunspots as usual.

Why is it important for us to know that? If sunspots could change the climate back then, they could do it now too. Then maybe we shouldn't just be blaming CO_2, but also the sun. Quite a lot of people have pinned their hopes on this scenario. But unfortunately, during an active period of the sun, there is a temperature increase of 0.1 of a degree at most. And a lazy period for the sun doesn't even cause a temperature drop of 0.1 of a degree. So sunspots don't have much to do with the Little Ice Age or with the warming that is taking place now.

This is also reflected, by the way, in the most recent data about sunspots and the temperature. Over the past decades, the sun has appeared to be getting less and less active. But the temperature just keeps on rising.

3 Air Bubbles & Tree Rings

In which you will read... why you already know more than an 18th-century geologist • why there are scratches on the mountains • how a scientist gets over a broken heart • how the Earth breathes in and out • how to make a hockey stick out of tree rings • what ancient air bubbles can tell us • how fingerprints give the culprit away.

In short: about research into climate change.

Time for Some Research

Two hundred years ago, people did not know more or less everything that you have read so far. Until the 18th century, European scientists didn't do much research into the Earth and the climate. They believed that the entire story of our planet was already in the Bible. So there wasn't that much more left to research.

God had created the Earth, around 6,000 years ago. The Irish archbishop James Ussher had worked it all out himself. On Saturday, October 22, in the year 4004 before Christ, at six o'clock in the evening, God created Heaven and Earth. You might laugh, but Ussher had taken a very serious approach to figuring it all out. He had looked at Bible stories and compared them with historical events, such as a lunar eclipse and the death of a famous king. And everything must have begun in October, of course, because otherwise there would have been no apples for Eve to take a bite out of.

After a while, the Great Flood happened. You know, the story of Noah in the ark with all kinds of animals, because God had flooded the world. This, of course, explained all those bones and fossils in the ground. They must belong to the animals that Noah had been unable to save.

But in the 18th century, miners went digging deeper and deeper into the Earth, in search of coal to fire steam engines. Geologists saw that the Earth consisted of layers, each with its own sort of stone and with different kinds of fossils. However, these layers were not always neat and straight.

James Ussher
1581-1656
archbishop

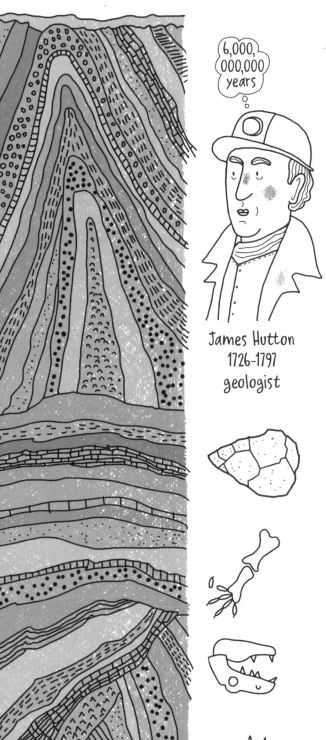

James Hutton
1726-1797
geologist

That could only mean that there had been other disasters like the Great Flood. But now the Earth was finished, or so they thought.

The Scottish scientist James Hutton had a very different opinion about all of this. Those layers had developed one by one. They were pushed together, crumpling and wearing down. The same forces made mountains appear and disappear, in the past and still today. Lots and lots of time was required for this to happen, of course. Far more than the 6,000 years that Archbishop Ussher had calculated.

Scientists like Hutton found it very difficult to sell their ideas to other people. They were living in a religious age and most scholars assumed that the Bible was completely correct. But gradually, more scientists came along with new theories. Theories that indicated the world was very old indeed. There was Charles Darwin, for instance, who discovered that animals and plants developed very slowly from other species. Many millions of years were needed for that to happen.

More and more people began to think that the Earth was maybe older, and that the Bible was not telling the whole story. They became curious about how exactly the world worked. Who did those giant bones in the ground belong to? How far away are the stars? And where did those strange stones come from?

Wandering Stones

In North America, Russia, and northern Europe, you can find wandering stones all over the place. They are more commonly known as glacial erratics. These are big boulders that don't actually belong where they are found. Some of them are bigger than a car and 20 times as heavy. The Big Rock erratic near Okotoks, Alberta, is the size of a two-story house. There's no mountain nearby that this stone could have come from. And that's rather strange.

It's normal to come across boulders like these in mountainous regions. They're just pieces of rock that have crumbled away from a mountain. When rivers are flowing quickly enough, the stones can hitch a quick ride and end up somewhere downstream. But when the water's calmer, it can only carry gravel and sand. Yet even in countries with no rocks or mountains whatsoever you can still find plenty of large stones that came from mountains. The biggest ones are sometimes nicely presented on town squares, with a helpful information board next to them.

There are lots of stories about these mysterious wandering stones. People say that the devil carried them there. Or that they grew out of the ground, all by themselves. Or that babies come from underneath them. Or that fighting trolls threw them at one another. And giants stacked them up to make megalithic monuments. This is all nonsense, of course. As is the story of the Great Flood, which many religious people used to explain the presence of these stones. But lots of scientists in those days wanted to believe the Bible. So they figured that icebergs had transported the boulders across the water. When the ice melted, the boulders were left behind. They didn't have the whole story down, but they were heading in the right direction.

In 1837, the Swiss geologist Louis Agassiz came up with the idea that the stones had been caught in big areas of glacial ice. These glaciers had carried the stones along for thousands of years and simply left them behind somewhere when they melted, often in a place where they'd never typically be found. This must have happened at a time when Europe was covered with big ice caps: an ice age. There was enough proof for this theory. In mountains, you can clearly see marks

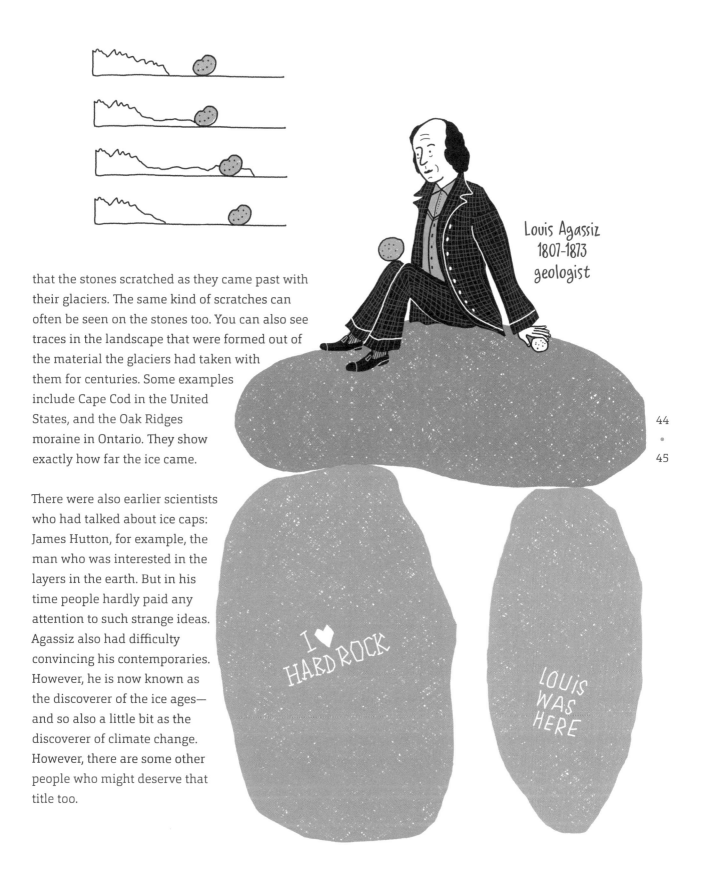

Louis Agassiz
1807–1873
geologist

that the stones scratched as they came past with their glaciers. The same kind of scratches can often be seen on the stones too. You can also see traces in the landscape that were formed out of the material the glaciers had taken with them for centuries. Some examples include Cape Cod in the United States, and the Oak Ridges moraine in Ontario. They show exactly how far the ice came.

There were also earlier scientists who had talked about ice caps: James Hutton, for example, the man who was interested in the layers in the earth. But in his time people hardly paid any attention to such strange ideas. Agassiz also had difficulty convincing his contemporaries. However, he is now known as the discoverer of the ice ages— and so also a little bit as the discoverer of climate change. However, there are some other people who might deserve that title too.

I ♥ HARD ROCK

LOUIS WAS HERE

The Discoverers of the Greenhouse

At the beginning of the 19th century, the French-man Joseph Fourier was racking his brains, trying very hard to work something out. How was it possible that Earth was not a much colder place? He took the size of the Earth and the distance from the sun and played around with the numbers a bit. He calculated that it should be, on average, 15 degrees below zero on Earth. But it was almost 15 degrees above zero. That could only mean that the Earth holds on to some of the heat of the sun. Fourier had discovered the greenhouse effect.

The atmosphere lets most of the rays of the sun come through to Earth. They only provide warmth when they hit the ground or your skin or something else. You can see this on a nice winter's day when you're out of the wind. The air is very cold, but the sun on your skin still feels warm. This happens because some of the rays have turned into rays of heat. And those rays don't get back out of the atmosphere as easily as the sun's rays entered. The atmosphere works in the same way as the glass in a greenhouse. Or in a car or a classroom, because it can get pretty hot there too. Rays of sun come in through the windows, change into rays of heat, and hang out for a while.

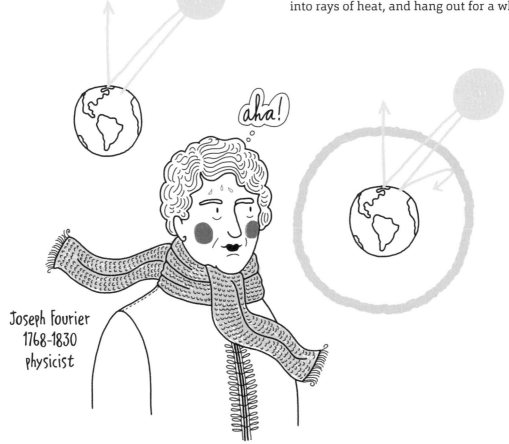

aha!

Joseph Fourier
1768-1830
physicist

It was another 70 years before someone else picked up on Fourier's ideas again. This was the Swedish physicist Svante Arrhenius. It was 1896 and the poor guy was broken-hearted: his marriage had hopelessly failed. So what do you do then if you're a brilliant scientist? You bury yourself in a mountain of numbers and you start calculating, day and night, until you find something spectacular. After a year, Arrhenius had got it: if there's half as much CO_2 in the air, the temperature will drop by five degrees. That's enough to cause an ice age.

But it also meant the opposite: if the amount of CO_2 doubles, then the temperature on Earth rises by five degrees. Looking back, those figures are a bit extreme. But Arrhenius was one of the first people to realize that, by burning coal, factories could release so much CO_2 into the air that it made the Earth warm up. This would further increase the greenhouse effect. So you could certainly call him the discoverer of our climate change.

As an inhabitant of the chilly country of Sweden, Arrhenius didn't have any objections to this warming effect, by the way. He was proud that, thanks to human activity, his children and grandchildren would have a milder climate. In a warmer climate, Swedish farmers would be able to grow much more food. He was just worried that the change would take a long time. As far as he was concerned, we should be burning more coal. And we did. But not because he said so.

COLD WITHOUT YOU CO_2

Svante Arrhenius
1859–1927
physicist

CO_2

The Breath of the Earth

FRESH AIR!

astronomers gazed up at the stars through telescopes on a nearby volcano, where factories and traffic jams did not get in the way. This was a good thing for Keeling too, as the amount of CO_2 in the air has to be measured very accurately.

When Keeling began, there were 315 particles of CO_2 to every million particles of air. The rest was made up of nitrogen, oxygen, and so on. So how did he know that there were 315 particles per million? He had to pump the air through a device with a special lamp. The lamp emits infrared radiation, just like a TV remote control. The more CO_2 there is in the air, the more radiation is blocked. A meter on one end of the device checks to see how much infrared is left. That's how they measure the amount of CO_2 in the air. This method also works for methane and other gases.

One fine day in 1958, the American chemist Charles Keeling drove up Mauna Loa, a volcano on Hawaii. It was quite a climb through a bare landscape of solidified lava. The research station where Keeling was going to work was at a height of 3,397 meters above sea level. He was going to measure how much CO_2 there was in the air. It was the ideal spot. At that altitude, far from civilization, the air is nice and pure. That was why

CO₂

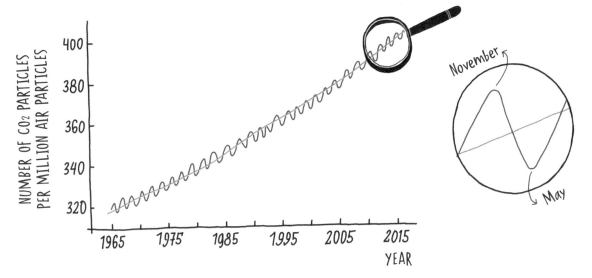

After a few years of measuring, Keeling discovered two important facts. The CO_2 in the air changes according to the season. From May, the amount of CO_2 drops, and from November it increases again. What Keeling was seeing was the breathing of the plants on Earth. In the Northern Hemisphere, to be precise, because there is much more land there and so more plants grow in the north than in the south of our planet. In springtime, the plants shoot up out of the ground and absorb a lot of CO_2. In the fall, lots of plants die, everything starts to decay, and the CO_2 goes back into the air. A graph can show you how the amount of CO_2 per million particles of air goes up and down in a wave: 315, 316, 317, 316, 315, 314, 313, 312, 313, 314, 315, 316, 317, 318, 317, 316, 315, 314, 313, 314, 315, 316, 317, 318, 319…

If you look closely at those figures, you can see the second important discovery that Keeling made. The peak of the waves is a little higher every year. In 1958, he measured an average of 315 particles of CO_2 per million, in 1959 it was 316, and in 1960 it was 317. Every year, it went up by about one particle per million. And this increase sped up. The levels of CO_2 are still measured on Mauna Loa today and now the number of particles of CO_2 in the air is increasing by more than two per year. As a result, on May 9, 2013, we passed 400 particles per million for the first time. And that figure just keeps on rising.

Svante Arrhenius would be happy to hear that there's so much CO_2. If his prediction is correct, it means the temperature on Earth should go up too.

Charles Keeling
1928-2005
chemist

48
·
49

The Growing Hockey Stick

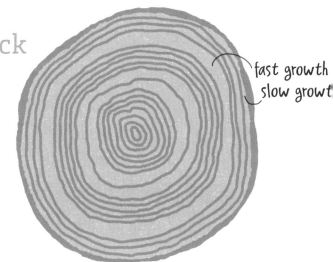

fast growth
slow growth

On the internet, you can quickly look up how hot it was on the day you were born, or on any other day in the past. Scientists began measuring and recording the temperature way back in 1706. But there are no figures from before that time. So how do we know how hot it was then? There are all kinds of sources for that information. They're not as reliable as a thermometer, but they're not far off.

You can look at tree rings, for example. The number of rings will tell you what age a tree reached. This works not only with trees that have just been cut down, but also with fossil trees that have been in the ground for thousands of years. You can tell from the rings whether a year was hot or cold, wet or dry. During a hot, wet summer, a tree grows faster and so the rings are thicker than in cold summers.

Researchers also drill into the ground, into the seabed, and into ice caps. This makes it possible for them to bring up details from long, long ago. The deeper you go, the older the material. It's just like in the laundry basket or a stack of comics: the oldest underpants and the oldest comics are at the bottom, because new ones keep getting piled on top.

At the end of the 20th century, the American Michael E. Mann and two of his colleagues made a graph that's become very famous. It shows the temperature over the past 1,000 years. In order to gauge the temperature, they researched thousands of tree rings. The graph became so famous that it had a nickname: the hockey stick. The stick is lying with its long side on the ground. That long side is the temperature in the years 1000 to 1900. It runs more or less in a straight line, with the temperature remaining about the same for 900 years. But from 1900 on, it goes up steeply. This is the blade of the hockey stick, the short part. For the last century, the temperature on Earth has risen quickly. And it has kept on going. The hockey stick is growing.

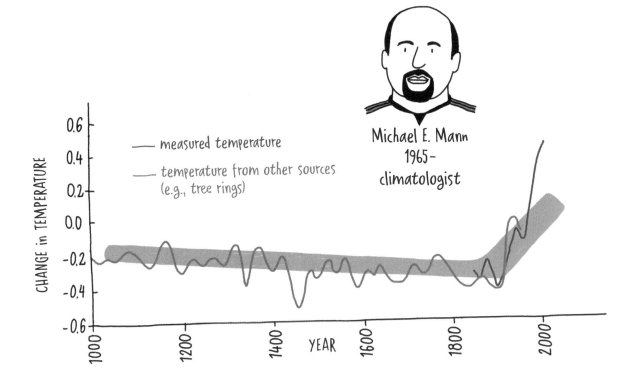

0.6
0.4
0.2
0.0
-0.2
-0.4
-0.6

CHANGE in TEMPERATURE

—— measured temperature

—— temperature from other sources
(e.g., tree rings)

Michael E. Mann
1965–
climatologist

1000   1200   1400   YEAR   1600   1800   2000

The creators of the graph received a lot of criticism. People thought they had not measured the changes properly. You couldn't even see that it was a bit warmer 1,000 years ago and a bit colder 500 years ago. So, 20 years later, they did their research again. Many more techniques for measuring even more precisely had come

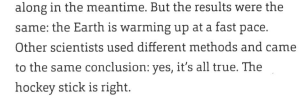

along in the meantime. But the results were the same: the Earth is warming up at a fast pace. Other scientists used different methods and came to the same conclusion: yes, it's all true. The hockey stick is right.

So the increase that you see in CO_2 can also be seen in the temperature. Arrhenius was right: the more CO_2 there is, the hotter it gets. But Keeling only went back to 1958, and the hockey stick only went back to the year 1000. However, we know that the climate can change a lot in the long term. So what were the temperature and the amount of CO_2 like long, long ago? You have to go into the cold to find that out.

Trapped in Ice

It's snowing in Antarctica. Fluffy snowflakes come fluttering down, not far from the South Pole. Every year, another thin layer is added to the snow. So the snowflakes end up lying deeper and deeper under other layers of snow. Tiny little bubbles of air in the snow are sealed off from the outside world. These bubbles contain oxygen, nitrogen, the breath of a mammoth, a pinch of salt from the sea, pollen, and ... CO_2. Year after year, those bubbles find themselves lying deeper and deeper under the snow. Snow falls in thick layers, compressing the snow below and turning it into ice. In every layer, air bubbles become trapped in the ice—and these air bubbles form the memory of the climate.

Eight hundred thousand years later, a team of researchers, all wrapped up warm, are standing beside an installation made of poles and cables. The wind is raw, the temperature is minus 40 degrees Celsius. Attached to the installation is a drill with a diameter of ten centimeters. One at a time, rods of ice are brought up to the surface, which the researchers then carefully pack up and carry away. They cut them into one-meter sections and write on a label what depth this ice came

from. The work continues like this for five years. The drill goes deeper than three kilometers. That's the depth of the ice that was created 800,000 years ago, with the bubbles of air still trapped inside.

The rods of ice go to a laboratory with a temperature of minus 35 degrees Celsius. There are metal tubes on the shelves in the ice-cold lab, containing rods that have been brought to the surface in different places in Greenland and Antarctica. Sometimes the scientists take one of these tubes off the shelves. Very carefully, they study the layers of ice. They melt little bits, releasing the air for the first time in hundreds of thousands of years. They capture this air in test tubes, and then the analysis can begin.

The scientists obtain a wealth of information from the rods of ice. Differences between the summer snow and the winter snow make it possible to tell the years apart by looking at the layers. The grains of pollen show which plants were in bloom at that time. If there's a lot of salt in the bubbles of air, you know there was a lot of wind coming off the sea that year. Remains of ash from volcanic eruptions tell you which volcanoes were active. But the most important factors for us are the temperature and the amount of CO_2.

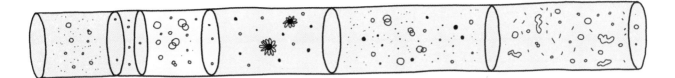

You can measure the amount of CO_2 in the air in the same way as Keeling did. The temperature in the past is trickier to find out; that has not been preserved in the ice. The thickness of the layers of snow does give us an idea of the temperature though. When it's very cold, less snow falls than when it's just a little bit cold, because heat is required to make water evaporate and form the clouds from which snow can fall. So thin layers of snow indicate colder times than thick layers of snow. But it's possible to be even more precise than that.

You can tell by the kind of oxygen in the bubbles of air if it was cold or warm on Earth at the time. Some particles of oxygen are a little lighter than others. Water with light oxygen particles evaporates more quickly than water with heavy oxygen particles. When it's colder, it's more difficult for water to evaporate, and so it's mainly light oxygen particles that find their way into the clouds and the snow. So if you find layers of ice with bubbles of air in them with lots of light oxygen particles and not many heavy particles, then they probably come from an ice age. It's all a bit complicated, isn't it?

Luckily, we can leave this sort of research to the experts. They could tell from the ice that for 800,000 years there was never more CO_2 in the air than 278 particles per million. So it's quite remarkable that we now suddenly have more than 400 particles per million. If you combine the increase in temperature and the increase in CO_2 in a graph, you'll see that they follow almost exactly the same pattern. If the CO_2 rises, then the temperature rises. And if the temperature rises, then the CO_2 rises. The dips in the graph are the ice ages. The peaks are the warmer periods in between. And right at the end, in the last two centuries, you can see the CO_2 rising to record levels. The temperature rises too, but less quickly. This is because it's more difficult to measure and because the oceans absorb a lot of heat. The last two centuries are the centuries when lots and lots more human beings came along on the Earth, and all of us pumped loads and loads of CO_2 into the air—with all our factories, cars, airplanes, and so on. So the rising temperatures must be our fault, wouldn't you think? But is that actually true?

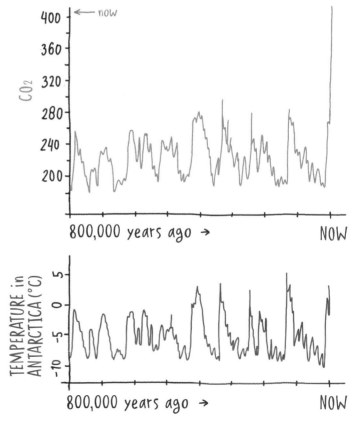

The Fingerprint of CO$_2$

OW!

People sometimes ask which came first, the chicken or the egg. What a silly question. It was the egg, of course! Dinosaurs were already laying eggs back in the days before there were any chickens around. But okay, what they mean is that the chicken comes out of an egg, and the egg comes out of a chicken. So how did it all begin?

You could ask yourself the same question about the rise in CO$_2$ and the rise in the temperature. You've seen in the graphs that they nearly always increase in the same way. Most scientists say that the higher temperatures are a result of the increased amount of CO$_2$ in the air. But couldn't it be the other way around? Might it not be the case that the Earth just happens to be warming up and that, as a result, more CO$_2$ is entering the air? So it's not our fault then, but, say, the power of the sun, the position of the planets, or the currents in the ocean.

If you zoom in on a graph of CO$_2$ and temperature in the ice ages, then you will in fact see that the CO$_2$ often lags a little behind the temperature. At the beginning of an ice age, you first see the temperature go down and then, after that, the amount of CO$_2$. But yes: ice ages are not caused by less CO$_2$ in the air. The temperatures change because of the position of the Earth relative to the sun. When it gets colder, CO$_2$ also disappears from the air, making it even colder. So the amount of CO$_2$ in the air can be both the cause and the consequence of changing temperatures. Just like a chicken can come out of an egg—and an egg can come out of a chicken.

CO$_2$

temperature

CO$_2$

CO$_2$

yes yes yes yes definitely yes yes yes yes yes yes yes yes yes yes yes yes yes yes yes yes no yes yes yes yes yes yes yes yes yes yes yes yes yes yes yes yes yes yes yes yes yes yes yes yes yes yes yes yes yes yes yes yes nope yes yes yes yes yes yes yes yes yes yes yes yes yes yes yes yes yes yes nah yes yes yes yes yes yes yes yes yeah yes yes yes yes yes yes yes yes yes yes yes

In graphs for the past few centuries, the lines for CO_2 and temperature dance happily around each other. More CO_2 causes warming, and warming causes more CO_2. But how do we know for certain that the extra CO_2 comes from chimneys and exhaust pipes, and not, for example, from the oceans or volcanoes? Well, there's plenty of evidence. In the Northern Hemisphere, the increase in CO_2 is always two years ahead of the CO_2 increase in the Southern Hemisphere. Two years is exactly the amount of time that CO_2 takes to spread out over the planet. So it seems that most of the CO_2 is emitted in the Northern Hemisphere. And that happens to be the half of the Earth where most of the people, factories, and cars are to be found. So it's right.

But there's even stronger evidence: the CO_2 has a sort of fingerprint. As with oxygen, you have light and heavy sorts of CO_2. Plants particularly like the lighter sort. So they absorb lots of light CO_2, and more heavy CO_2 is left behind in the air. This means that there's naturally a little more light CO_2 in plants and a little more heavy CO_2 in the air. However, since the 18th century this has been changing. There has been more and more light CO_2 in the air. This is released when coal, gas, and oil are burned, because those fuels are made of plants. At the same time, there is less and less oxygen in the air. This is also a big clue—because oxygen is needed to burn coal, gas, and oil. And it's not needed for other sources of CO_2, such as volcanoes and oceans.

Ninety-seven percent of climate scientists are convinced that the climate change that is taking place now is caused by human beings. They have other forms of proof for this, which are even more complicated than what you just read. Everything indicates that global warming is happening because of the extra CO_2 from chimneys and exhaust pipes. But they're not the only factors that are changing the climate. Trees and cows also have a lot to answer for.

4 Chimneys & Cow Farts

In which you will read... where our forests went • who Watt was • about the thing about coal • why there are skyscrapers in the middle of the desert • how many more people a day arrive on Earth • that your electricity comes from steam too • why oil is thick and gasoline is thin • why cows look so innocent.

In short: about the causes of climate change.

Wood

Ever since the last few ice ages, humans have been interfering with the climate. Until that time, only nature had an influence on the amount of CO_2 in the air. But roughly 400,000 years ago, people first started to make campfires. Can you blame them, what with the cold and all those wolves on the prowl?

Making fires sent all the carbon that was in those trees into the air as CO_2. More forest fires happened too. Maybe by accident, when a spark blew into a dry forest. Or maybe intentionally, because the prehistoric people wanted to create open plains where they could hunt wild animals more easily. Whatever the case, archeologists have found layers of charcoal in the ground that date back to the last ice age and prove that there were big forest fires at the time. Forest fires like that send a load of CO_2 into the air and also destroy trees that can absorb CO_2—as is happening in the 21st century in Australia, Canada, Brazil, Indonesia, the United States, and other countries, and as happened in recent centuries in Europe, Asia, and North America.

What do you think it looked like in central and eastern North America around 5,000 years ago? It was all forest as far as you could see. Look in front of you, look behind you, look left, look right. There were trees everywhere, even in the swamps that were around back then. There were ferns, fungi, and moss growing among the trees, and beetles, mice, and foxes scuttling around. There were forests where now there are schools, skate parks, supermarkets, and sports stadiums. So where did they go?

Most of the trees were used for construction. The first houses, ships, roads: they were all made from wood. People had no problem cutting down the forest or burning it to the ground. Quite the opposite, in fact. The forest was dark, and it was full of scary animals and mean robbers. Down with the forest!

For centuries, wood was the most important material for villages and cities. Even after brick houses came along, wood was still necessary. You make brick by baking clay in an oven, which you power by burning ... wood. The blacksmith needed wood for his fire too, and so did the baker and the glassblower and so on and so on.

Wherever big cities developed, the forests disappeared. So wealthy cities and countries had to fetch their wood from faraway places, just like we bring oil from distant countries nowadays. In the 17th century, when the Netherlands was experiencing an economic boom, the country imported its wood from Scandinavia and Germany. In those days, you could see rafts on the Rhine that were the length of high-speed trains. They were made of German tree trunks heading for the prosperous Netherlands.

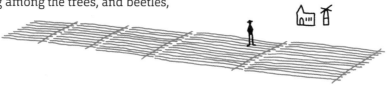

Until the 19th century, this made wood the biggest source of extra CO_2. If you look inside ice rods, you'll find that air bubbles from the 17th century, the period of the economic boom, contain just a little bit more CO_2 than ones from when the knights were still around, which have more than the ones from the Roman era, which have more than the ones from prehistoric times. But the increase isn't too dramatic. At the beginning of the 19th century, "only" one billion people lived on our planet. Seven times less than now. And the Industrial Revolution had only just begun.

The Water-Vapor Engine

Put a pan of water on the heat and after a while the lid will start to rattle up and down. This is because the water is turning into vapor, and water vapor, or steam, takes up more room than liquid water. So the steam is pushing against the lid because it wants to escape. This is how heat causes movement. This simple trick is the basis of the steam engine. And the steam engine was the basis of the Industrial Revolution. It could just as easily be called the water-vapor engine, because water vapor and steam are the same thing.

fire + water → water vapor

Still, you can't use a pan of water to make a steam train run or to power a weaving machine. Fortunately, there were inventors around who understood how these kinds of things worked, and they kept on tinkering away until they'd invented a decent steam engine. Around 250 years ago, James Watt figured it out: a steam machine that provided enough power to take over the heavy work done by humans and horses.

horsepower

James Watt was from Scotland, and so the Industrial Revolution began in Great Britain. As a result of new agricultural techniques, the population there grew quickly. It was almost impossible to spin yarn, weave fabric, and make clothes for everyone by hand. But, after the invention of the steam engine, they had weaving machines and spinning machines that were powered by steam. These were a big success. More and more factories were built, with more and more machines—in Great Britain and later in the rest of Europe, in America, and in Asia.

The steam engine was a truly amazing invention. Before it came along, people had only wind, water, and muscle power to get things moving. Windmills pumped away water to make new land, called polders. Watermills milled grain. Horses pulled carts. And people wove fabrics by hand. The steam engine could do all of that better and faster. And the steam engine never got tired. You just had to make sure that there was enough fuel to heat the water. That fuel was coal, because they had almost run out of wood.

The people took coal out of the ground. First from places where it was not too deep, because otherwise the water in the ground could cause problems. But the invention of the steam engine allowed them to go deeper. The steam engine pumped the groundwater out of the mine. So now the miners could fetch the coal from a depth of kilometers. This coal had been trapped down there for around 300 million years.

Mashed Marsh Plants

Let's go back 300 million years in time, to the age of the big scary critters. There is no sign of any dinosaurs yet. Much of the world is covered with trees, plants, leaves. It is hot and humid, like a tropical swimming paradise. The swamp is full of ferns and strange plants with what looks like feathers for leaves. Insects are buzzing all around. Now and then, one of the first reptiles snatches a bug from the air. They have to watch out for the *Meganeura* though. That's a giant dragonfly with wings the size of a magpie's.

We know about the *Meganeura* because a fossil of one was found deep inside a French coal mine. It is quite amazing that an insect with such delicate wings was preserved for 300 million years. Most of the other giant dragonflies were eaten up or rotted away. But this *Meganeura* must have fallen into a swamp after its death, where there were no fish to eat it. That's quite likely, as lots of swamps contain hardly any oxygen. That meant that the dragonfly didn't rot when it sank to the bottom. It's a miracle that the dragonfly wasn't crushed and crumpled. Thousands of them probably ended up at the bottom of the swamp, with just a few remaining so wonderfully intact.

The dragonflies disappeared among the dead trees, plants, and leaves that also ended up in the swamp. All of this deposited a huge load of carbon in the ground, which sank deeper and deeper. Very slowly, a sort of sponge made up of dead plant matter developed in the water: peat. If you dry peat, you can use it as fuel—which makes sense, because it's made up of wood and plants. We use wood as fuel, for example in campfires. We also use plants as fuel, like when you eat sprouts or spinach. Your body burns them and they give you energy. Wood and plants also contain energy. The more carbon they contain, the more energy they have. And that's the thing about coal.

Coal is super-compressed peat. Over millions of years, the peat ended up deeper and deeper in the earth, where it's much hotter. Thick layers of sand and clay formed on top of it, and dinosaurs stomped around on it. There have been times when there were seas above it. All those layers pressed the peat more and more tightly together, squeezing the water and oxygen out of it and making it harder and harder. More and more carbon was left, and therefore more energy. Think about it: a layer of 10 meters of coal

swamp

remains of plants

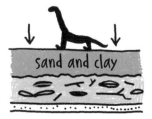

sand and clay

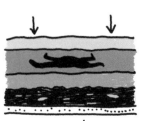

coal

was once a layer of 100 meters of peat. That's why a kilogram of coal burns longer than a kilo of peat and even longer than a kilo of wood.

Plants disappeared under the ground like this in many places on Earth. Not only 300 million years ago, but also before and after, and it's still happening now. But in the age of the *Meganeura*, there were lots and lots of forests that disappeared into the swamps for a very long time and which are now being brought back to the surface as coal.

The coal contains lots of fossils, mainly of ferns and other plants. And very occasionally of a prehistoric creature like the *Meganeura*. So that's why we call fuels such as coal "fossil fuels." There are two other fossil fuels: oil and natural gas.

PLANKTON
fish food

Crushed Sea Creatures

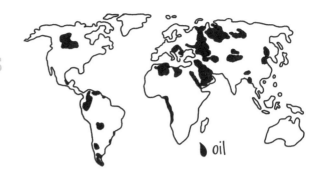

oil

Oil is distributed over the planet less fairly than coal. In countries like Kuwait and Saudi Arabia, they don't mind that at all. The ground there is so full of oil that they sell nearly all of it to other countries for lots and lots of dollars. They use that money to build the highest skyscrapers, the most expensive stores, and the most modern museums, all in the middle of the desert.

Two hundred million years ago, there was a big shallow ocean in this region. The water was packed with fish, lobsters, shrimp, and plankton. When they died, the sea creatures sank to the bottom, where they were covered with sand and clay, so they didn't start to rot. This went on for millions of years. The creatures sank deeper and deeper. As with the peat, they were pressed more and more tightly together, and as with the coal there was basically only carbon left. But because there were fewer plants involved and because the whole mess was deeper, and therefore hotter, it was in a liquid form: oil.

In places where there is oil or coal, natural gas is sometimes found too. Natural gas is actually just methane from the earth. It develops when oil or coal is heated a lot, which happens sometimes because oil and coal are often under kilometers of thick layers of stone, where the temperature can easily reach 100 degrees Celsius. Then methane comes out of the remains of the animals and plants. Like every gas, methane rises. Most of it seeps through cracks and holes in the earth and escapes into the atmosphere. But sometimes it hits a layer of earth that it can't pass through. Then the gas remains trapped in small pockets in the ground.

So, scattered all around the world, there are thick layers of carbon in the ground. Carbon in a solid form (coal), in a liquid form (oil), and in the form of gas (natural gas). The carbon comes from animals and plants, many of which have been dead for hundreds of millions of years. If they hadn't ended up in shallow seas and swamps, they would have been eaten up or rotted away. Then, little by little, all the CO_2 would have gone up into the air. But that didn't happen. Beneath our feet, there's a huge supply of carbon that nature built up over millions of years—and we're now racing through it in just a few centuries.

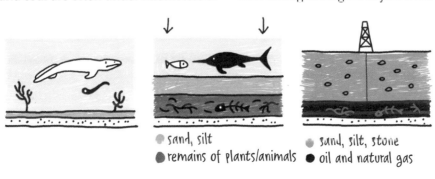

sand, silt
remains of plants/animals

sand, silt, stone
oil and natural gas

People, People Everywhere

In the days of James Watt, a billion people lived on Earth. That's 1,000 times 1,000 times 1,000 people. People traveled by horse and cart. There was no such thing as cars. The steam train had just been invented. Lots of people lived in big families in small, cramped houses. There was no toilet and no water supply. Contagious diseases seized their chance via the poop bucket and the water pump. People were more likely to become ill and, if they were ill, more likely to die, as there weren't many effective medicines.

It took another 123 years before there were two billion inhabitants of Earth. That was in 1927. Your grandma's grandma was probably still alive back then. Cars and horses and carts traveled the streets together. More and more houses had a toilet that was connected to the sewer. Antibiotics were discovered: medicines that meant simple diseases no longer had to be fatal. From that point on, the world's population grew faster and faster.

Less than a hundred years later, we already have more than 7.5 billion people. Those people combined have more than a billion cars, 1.5 billion TVs, and 7 billion telephones. All those cars use fuel. All those devices use electricity. All those people have to eat and drink. And more and more people are coming along all the time.

It's hard to predict how quickly the population will grow in the future. In the time it took you to read this sentence, 30 people were born and 10 people died. And so an extra 200,000 people join our world population every day. If this continues, we'll have 11 billion inhabitants in 2050 and 17 billion in 2100. But it seems that women are, on average, having fewer children. So you probably don't have as many brothers and sisters as your grandmother and grandfather had. If that trend continues, there'll be 9.5 billion inhabitants of Earth in 2050 and 11 billion in 2100—which is still a lot.

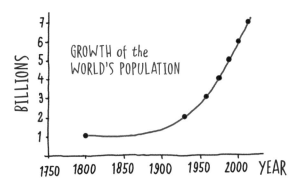

So there are more and more people who have to eat and drink. And more and more clothes and houses are needed. But do you know what really is a problem? People are getting older and richer. That's all very nice, of course, but those long and luxurious lives consume a lot of energy. Because rich people use a lot of machines and gadgets, go on a lot of vacations, have one or two cars, and buy new things all the time.

Probably you are also rich, certainly compared to the rest of the world. Luckily, the rest of the world

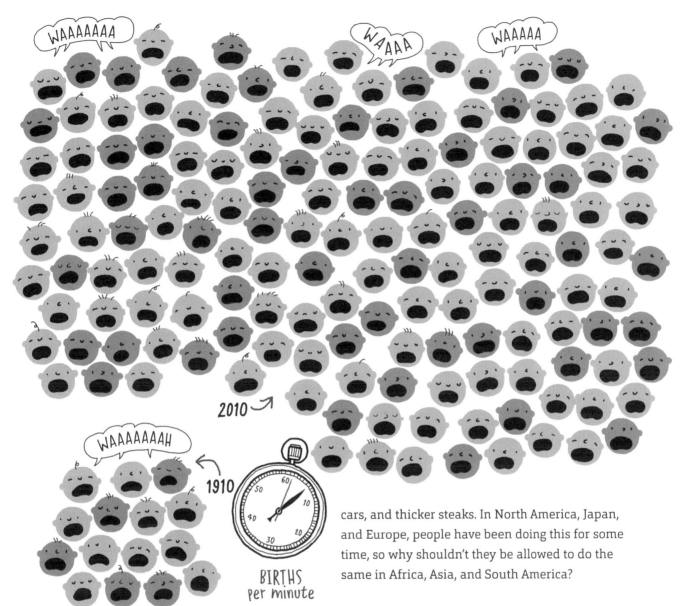

cars, and thicker steaks. In North America, Japan, and Europe, people have been doing this for some time, so why shouldn't they be allowed to do the same in Africa, Asia, and South America?

All those houses, factories, and offices have to be built, of course. The lighting has to work, the air-conditioning has to function—everyone wants electricity. All the cars need to drive, the planes need to fly, the ships need to sail. That all uses gasoline, kerosene, gas, oil. And all the people need to eat. Meat, fish, grain, vegetables. That uses energy and makes a lot of farts and burps. So more and more greenhouse gases come out of the chimneys, the exhaust pipes, and the cows.

is also becoming richer. In that respect, our planet is doing fantastically well. Countries such as China, Brazil, and South Africa were much poorer 30 years ago than they are now. In recent years, they've been catching up quickly. They're just a bit late to the Industrial Revolution. But now there are factories and offices everywhere. There's more work, people are earning more money, and so they're buying bigger houses, more expensive

Out of the Chimney

Sometimes it goes wrong. Then all the lights suddenly go off. The computer stops working, the fridge stops buzzing, and the heating slowly cools down. "How long is this going to last?" you wonder. But the Wi-Fi's not working either, so you can't find out. Outside, you see that the streetlights, the streetcars, and the traffic lights have given up too. Yep, it's definitely a real power outage. You'd better light some candles.

A hundred years ago, this would never have happened. The streetlights were powered by gas, horses pulled the streetcars, and a police officer directed the traffic. Inside, the wood fire was burning, oil lamps provided the light, and there were no screens. You'll only know what that feels like if you've ever experienced a major power failure. You're used to using a button or a switch or a plug to turn on all kinds of devices. The funny thing is that most of these machines are still actually powered by steam engines.

The electricity in your wall socket comes from a power station. And many power stations use coal to power a kind of steam engine. The coal is ground up into powder and then burned under a huge boiler of water. The gases that are left disappear through filters and out of the chimney into the air. Those filters block all kinds of things, but not the CO_2.

Steam is created inside the boiler. That takes up much more room than water, and so it wants to get out of there as quickly as possible. With that power, the steam drives a turbine, a sort of super-deluxe mill. Up to this point, not much happens differently than in a steam engine: heat is converted into movement. Now that movement just has to become electricity. This happens in a generator.

Like a mechanical flashlight or a bicycle dynamo, the generator converts movement into electricity. This electricity passes through all sorts of different stages to get to your house, where it calmly waits for you inside the wall sockets. As soon as you put in a plug, the electricity starts to run through the cable, and you can charge your phone.

All over the world, there are tens of thousands of power stations like that, but most of them are actually glorified steam engines. The only difference is in the way they heat the water. Some of them do this without fossil fuels. They can be powered by nuclear energy or geothermal energy. But most burn coal, gas, or oil.

This finally releases the carbon formed from trees, ferns, and dragonflies 300 million years ago in a swamp. Together with some other gases, the CO_2 goes out through the chimney and into the air.

Out of the Exhaust Pipe

Do you know the smell of plane engines? You can sometimes smell them just as you're exiting the aircraft, particularly if you're leaving by the stairs. That smell is completely different from the smell of a cruise ship or the smell of a gas station. This is because planes are powered by kerosene, ships sail on fuel oil, and most cars run on gasoline or diesel. All of those fuels are extracted from oil—and that's not an easy task.

Oil is a dirty syrupy gloop when it comes out of the ground, as you realize when you see photographs of oil disasters—for example, when there's an explosion on a drilling rig or when an oil tanker leaks. Millions of liters of thick oil flow into the sea. You see pictures on the TV news of pelicans trapped in a thick layer of black gunge, crabs peeping out above the oil, and volunteers struggling to scrub the sea turtles clean.

This oil travels on ships and along pipelines to oil refineries. The oil is called "crude oil" because it's still a thick mixture that's not much good to anyone. At the refinery, they separate the various parts of the mixture by heating it. You can take apart salty water in more or less the same way. (Put some salty water in a pan. Place it on the heat. Allow the water to boil away until the salt crystallizes. Hold a spoon or something similar in the steam. Let it cool and then taste the drops of water. No sign of salt!) But it's a bit more complicated than that, and it happens inside a really tall boiler with all kinds of interesting pipes. The lowest pipes pump fuel oil and diesel out of the boiler, and the higher pipes pump kerosene and gasoline. This is because the boiler is hotter at the bottom than at the top. The heaviest liquid stays at the bottom. The lightest rises highest.

The different fuels have different qualities. Gasoline is handy if you want to start an engine quickly. There's more energy in a liter of kerosene than in a liter of gasoline. Fuel oil is less flammable than gasoline. This is why most cars run on gasoline, most planes fly on kerosene, and most ships sail on fuel oil.

They need these fuels to power the engine. Inside an engine, little explosions are constantly taking place. They happen because a mixture of air and fuel is ignited by a spark. The power of the explosion pushes a piston, just like you when you step on your bike pedals. This sets the wheels or the propellers in motion.

Burning the fuel finally sets free the carbon formed in the sea 200 million years ago out of shells and plankton. Together with some other gases, the CO_2 goes out through the exhaust pipe and into the air.

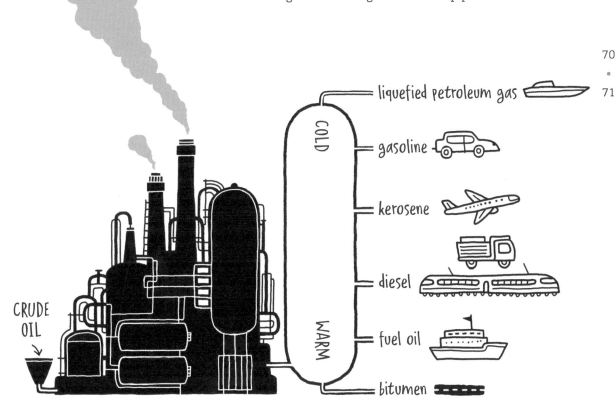

CRUDE OIL

COLD

WARM

liquefied petroleum gas

gasoline

kerosene

diesel

fuel oil

bitumen

Out of the Cow

Cows can look very innocent as they stand there ruminating in the field. They gaze a bit dozily into the distance, looking as if butter wouldn't melt in their mouths. Meanwhile, they're contributing to climate change just as much as the average car. They do this by emitting not CO_2 but methane, one of the other major greenhouse gases. Methane is about 25 times stronger than CO_2. Luckily it doesn't hang around in the air for as long.

Methane is in natural gas, in swamps, and in cows' burps. Their burps are much worse than their farts. But when cow poo begins to rot, it also releases a whole load of methane. The cows burp so much methane because they have four stomachs. They use those stomachs to digest the grass they eat. That grass contains a lot of carbon. All kinds of bacteria help out during digestion, and some of them make methane gas out of the grass. Cows burp out the methane. And they don't even say "Excuse me!"

Now, it's not really the cows' fault either. And it's not even the fault of the bacteria. It's because people eat so many hamburgers and drink so much milk. Otherwise there wouldn't be nearly as many cows. And nowhere near as many sheep or goats. Because they're pretty gassy too. All ruminants (animals that have a complicated digestive system with a three- or four-chambered stomach) are champion burpers, in fact. And that includes camels, giraffes, deer, and all the rest. But there are a billion cows on the planet, and that's because humans breed so many of them.

Burping beasties are not the only bad guys of agriculture. The bacteria that make methane are crazy about rice fields too. That's where around a quarter of the methane in the atmosphere comes from. Some scientists even say that climate change began when people started to cultivate rice, 8,000 years ago. Amounts of methane found in ice with air bubbles from that time seem to indicate that this is the case.

And then there's another thing. A lot of land is needed to grow food and to keep animals and to grow food for those animals. More and more land. Because there are more and more people, and those people are getting richer and richer, and they want to eat more and more. That's why chainsaws are ringing out in tropical woodland and why forest fires are blazing away. Millions of trees have been felled to make more room for agriculture. For soybeans, for instance, which are used in soybean oil, soy sauce, and often as cattle feed. Felling trees creates a double problem. The carbon in the wood goes into the air as CO_2. And fewer trees remain to take the CO_2 back out of the air.

5 Meltwater & Heat Waves

In which you will read... what the climate is again • why scientists need more pages than I do • why the North Pole is melting faster than the South Pole • that the Great Lakes are at the bottom of a seesaw • how thousands of plastic ducks helped ocean science • which robots get a dunking every 10 days • why you'd better keep more of an eye out for hailstones • what happens when the freezer defrosts • about tipping points and time bombs.

In short: about the consequences of climate change.

Climate Confusion

In southern Australia, there is a region full of abandoned farms. There's not much more left of most of them than a few collapsing walls. The farms were built sometime around 1865, and people didn't live in them for very long. The farmers had only just come to Australia, and they didn't know the land very well yet. All they knew was that it was very dry in the middle of the country and that there was more rain close to the sea. So a land surveyor was called in to investigate the areas that were suitable for agriculture. His name was George Goyder. He went out to explore and after a while he drew a clear line on the map. To the north of this line, it's too dry for agriculture, he said. But to the south of that line, you're safe to start a farm.

Goyder had hardly spoken when the rain came pouring from the sky—including to the north of that line he had drawn. The stubborn farmers had seen all they needed to see. They built their farms far inland—in the region where, according to Goyder, it was far too dry for agriculture. The harvest was good that year. But in the years that followed, Goyder was proved right. One after another, the farmers left their land and headed south. Enough rain fell there almost every year for a good harvest.

The farmers had made a foolish mistake. They were confusing the weather with the climate. If it rains or snows somewhere one day, that doesn't mean it always rains or snows there. The weather varies from one minute to the next, but the climate does not. The weather is about the temperature and the precipitation at a particular moment. The climate is about the average weather over a period of at least 30 years. It's just like with people, really. You can be a very happy person by nature, but sometimes you're just in a bad mood. The climate is like your character. The weather is like your mood.

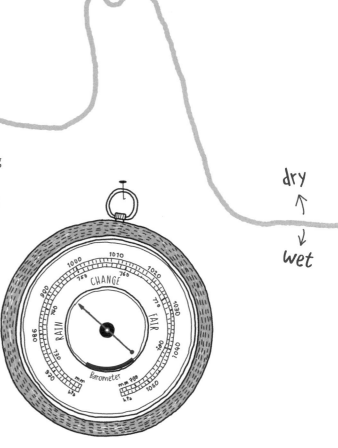

dry

wet

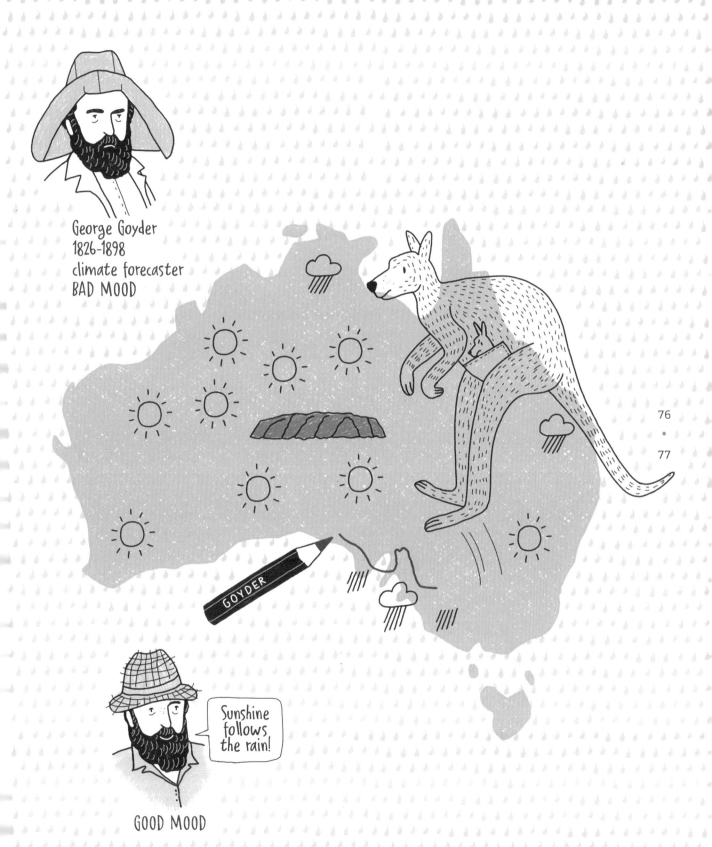

George Goyder
1826-1898
climate forecaster
BAD MOOD

GOYDER

Sunshine follows the rain!

GOOD MOOD

One Degree Warmer

"Hottest Year Ever Measured," "Driest November," "Longest Heat Wave." One weather record after another has fallen in recent years. That, in itself, does not say anything about the climate, just about the weather. A bizarrely warm winter or a really weird hailstorm can happen even without climate change. But when lots of those things happen often, then it does seem as if there's something going on.

Compare it to dice. Sure you can throw a six three times in a row. With every throw, you have the same chance of a six as the previous throw. But if you keep on throwing one six after another, then it becomes suspicious. Hey, you can buy weighted dice at a toy store for a couple of dollars.

Someone who throws a six a few times in a row isn't necessarily a cheat. But if they go on throwing sixes, then it might make you think that maybe they are cheating. In the same way, not every weather record is necessarily the fault of climate change. But when you have so many new records in a row, then there has to be something going on.

At the moment, the average temperature around the world is over one degree higher than in 1850. You think that doesn't sound like much? Then think back to the hockey stick. Over the past

thousand years, the temperature has fluctuated around 13.5 degrees Celsius. Sometimes it was 13.3, sometimes 13.6. But it stayed pretty much the same. Tree rings and air bubbles inside ice rods show that it remained around 13.5 degrees for at least 10,000 years. So, compared to that, an increase of one degree in less than 200 years is ridiculously high. And in recent years, that increase has been speeding up. If it continues, it'll take only 50 years to add another degree.

Once every five or six years, a thick report comes out, published by the IPCC, the Intergovernmental Panel on Climate Change. This is a group of thousands of scientists from all over the world who do research into climate change. The scientists certainly don't agree about everything, but they do have to write a report together. The result is a kind of average of their conclusions. If a whole load of countries say "climate change is definitely the result of human activity" and a few countries say "climate change may be the result of human activity," then the conclusion will be that "climate change is most likely the result of human activity."

The last IPCC report was almost 5,000 pages long. In it, the scientists say that, by the end of the century, the Earth will certainly be 1.5 degrees warmer than in 1850—even if we seal up all the chimneys, exhaust pipes, and cows right now, which is obviously not going to happen. But it might be possible to limit the increase to two degrees. We'll all have to work hard to do it though: close coal-fired power stations, build wind turbines, and eat fewer hamburgers. If we don't do anything at all and just keep on burning coal and cutting down trees, then in 2100 we'll be four degrees hotter than in 1850.

From 13.5 degrees to 17.5 in two and a half centuries. Then the hockey stick is growing really quickly. The climate has often changed in the past, but never that fast. So the consequences of an increase of four degrees are impossible to predict. And that increase is just an average. Some places will warm up less, and so there will also be places where the temperature goes up by even more than four degrees.

But hey, it's not 2100 yet. So there's a good chance that the increase will be somewhere between 1.5 and 4 degrees. You can already see the consequences though: glaciers are melting, the sea level is rising, the weather is acting strangely.   And that's just the beginning.

IT IS!

IT ISN'T!

CATASTROPHIC

IT'LL BE OKAY

written by thousands of scientists

5,000 pages?! That's half a tree!

CLIMATE CHANGE IPCC

Melting Poles

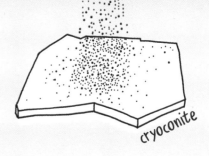

cryoconite

In Greenland, you can hear the climate changing. Drip drip drip. The sound of melting ice. Walk on a bit and you won't hear any more dripping. It'll be drowned out by rushing rivers that are carrying away the meltwater. With huge force, they carve a bright-blue path through the ice. Closer to the sea, you can hear the squeaking and creaking of sheets of ice. They break away from the glaciers and float quietly out into the ocean, where they slowly melt.

You can find glaciers wherever snow falls and it's cold enough for the snow to survive the summer. So that's around the North Pole and the South Pole. But also in other places, mainly in the mountains, because it can be cold enough there too. Maybe you've skied on glacier snow. Perhaps you've seen the photos of giraffes and elephants with the snowy Mount Kilimanjaro in the background, in the middle of Africa. Even there, not far from the equator, you can find glaciers. But for how much longer? All over the world, glaciers are shrinking. In Switzerland, Argentina, Tanzania, Nepal… This will have serious consequences. Billions of people use the glaciers as a water supply.

The largest ice packs are in Antarctica and Greenland. They have been there since the beginning of the ice ages, millions of years ago. In some places, the ice is three kilometers thick. There are entire mountain ranges buried beneath it. Every year, the layer of ice becomes a bit thinner. In the summer, more ice melts away than is added during the winter. This is, of course, because the temperature is rising. But there are all kinds of things that speed up the melting process. They have strange names like *moulins* and *cryoconite*.

Moulin is the French word for mill. These are big round holes in the ice, and the water flows into them and away, swirling around like a whirlpool. This takes the meltwater to the underside of the ice, which makes the ice melt faster and break up into pieces. That's how moulins speed up the melting of the glaciers. And cryoconite is the black stuff that you sometimes see in photographs of glaciers: a thin layer making all that beautiful snow look a bit grimy. The layer is made up of dust from deserts, ash from volcanoes, and soot from factories and cars. It's carried to the poles on the wind. The black areas absorb more heat than the white ice. This makes it melt faster and creates black holes in the ice. So that's another melting accelerator.

The North Pole's largest area of ice is in Greenland. But other countries around the Arctic Ocean are also partly covered with glaciers. The sea itself is frozen for much of the year. There is pack ice as far as you can see, like ice floes all frozen together. You've probably seen it in those photographs of lonely polar bears. Every summer, some of the

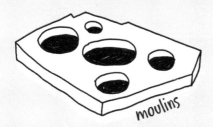

moulins

ice melts, and every winter it grows back. But because the summers and winters are becoming warmer, more and more ice is melting away and less ice is growing back. Some predictions say that the summer ice will disappear within a few years.

The North Pole region is unlucky. It's warming up much faster than other areas on Earth. For centuries, the sea ice worked as a protective layer against the heat. With its white color, the ice reflected the sunlight. Now that the ice is disappearing, the dark sea absorbs far more heat. The heat that was stored under the sea ice is also being released. It's not very warm, of course, but it's still warmer than the layer of ice above.

NORTH POLE

SOUTH POLE

The South Pole region is the opposite of the North Pole in almost every way. When it's summer at one, it's winter at the other. There are no polar bears at the South Pole, and there are no penguins at the North Pole. The South Pole is

land surrounded by sea, and the North Pole is sea surrounded by land. Antarctica would fit into the Arctic Ocean almost like a cork. Ice on land can grow a lot thicker, so there's ten times as much ice at the South Pole as at the North Pole. Together, the two poles contain more than 99 percent of all ice on Earth.

The South Pole is also much colder than the North Pole. That's because it's such a large land mass. There's much less sea to ease the cold a little. It's also pretty mountainous. If you've ever been to the mountains, you'll know it's a lot colder up there than in the valleys. The thick layer of ice in Antarctica makes the continent even higher and therefore even colder. On average, it's just as cold there in the summer as it is at the North Pole in the winter. Around 25 degrees below zero. In the winter, it can get down to minus 60. This also makes a difference to the freezing ice. If ice is going to melt there, Antarctica needs to heat up a lot! You do see large and small sheets of ice breaking off around the edge of the land though. That makes it easier for the glaciers behind them to slide into the sea too. These glaciers make the sea level rise, because they've come off the land.

Melting land ice makes the sea level rise. The water adds to the sea. Melting sea ice, though, makes no difference to the water level. Ice floes and sheets of ice are already floating on the water. Why don't you see for yourself what happens when they melt?

Weird Water

Put some ice cubes in a glass of water. Stick some tape at the exact height of the water level. The ice cubes should stick up above it. What will happen when the ice cubes melt? Will the water level rise, will it fall, or will it stay the same? Okaaay… This is going to take a while… You might as well go on reading in the meantime.

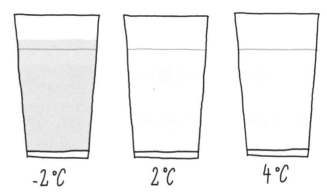

The ice cubes are just like ice floes and icebergs: they stick up a bit above the water, but most of them is below the surface. This is because ice takes up more room than water. When water freezes, there's more space between the water particles. This means that it expands and keeps floating. The amount of ice above the water is exactly the extra space that the water needs. When ice melts, that extra space is no longer needed and so the water level remains the same. Just take a look at your glass.

You can also do this experiment the other way around. Fill a sturdy plastic cup up to the brim with water. Put it in the freezer and wait until it's completely frozen. Now the ice will come up above the edge. Not a drop of water has been added and yet the water needs more space. If you let the ice melt, it will fit perfectly into the cup again. So when sea ice melts, it also has no effect on the sea level.

This is a strange feature of water. Almost every other substance shrinks and sinks when it goes from liquid to solid. Water expands and floats. But water has another peculiar feature, one that does have an influence on the sea level. In addition to taking up more space when it's frozen and solid, water also takes up more space when it's over four degrees. For every extra degree, the water expands a little more. This is true for all water at four degrees and warmer. So that's just about every ocean and sea then, to a depth of kilometers. The sea level rises not only because of melting land ice, but also because warmer water needs more space.

It is hard to predict how much the water will rise. There could come a point, for instance, when the melting of the Greenland ice cap can no longer be stopped. In that case, the entire layer of ice will disappear into the sea, and the sea level all over the world will go up by seven meters. This is not something that you will experience, unless you're taking immortality pills. In 2014, the IPCC thought the sea level would rise by a maximum of one meter this century. But there have since been reports that it could be double that. That's quite a difference—and it also matters where you live.

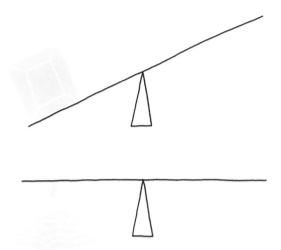

That's because the surface of the sea is not perfectly smooth. It's actually more of a hilly landscape, as a result of currents and also because of differences in gravitational force. Large land masses attract water, just as the Earth pulls at the moon and the sun pulls at the Earth. Even the ice caps of Greenland and Antarctica have so much mass that they pull water toward them. If the ice caps melt, that mass will decrease, and more water will go to other areas. The land will also rise a little, as there is less ice weighing it down. So Greenland and Antarctica themselves won't suffer too much because of the rising sea level.

There are other regions that rise and fall in relation to the sea. During the ice age, the north of Great Britain was covered with ice. Now that the ice is gone, Scotland has risen a little again. And, like on a seesaw, the south of the island has gone down a bit. Parts of Canada have also come back up a little, now that the heavy ice has disappeared. The east coast of the United States and the Great Lakes are on the other end of that seesaw. So the land there is sinking a bit.

Rivers in the Sea

They were heading across the water for some little adventures in American bathtubs. But on the way from China to the United States, their ship got caught in a serious storm. The container they were in was swept overboard, and the doors swung open. And there they were, bobbing around in the middle of the Pacific Ocean: almost 29,000 plastic bath toys. Yellow duckies, green frogs, red beavers, and blue turtles. More than 10 months later, a beachcomber on the coast of Alaska found the first 10 animals. Some of them looked a bit pale, but they'd survived.

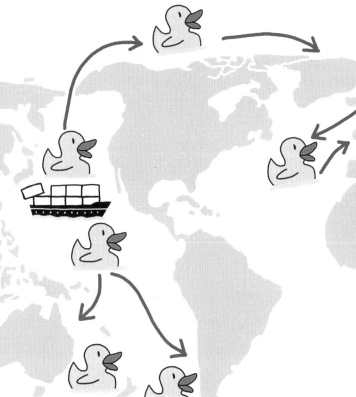

The oceanographer Curtis Ebbesmeyer knew at once that this was an excellent opportunity to find out more about the currents of the ocean. With thousands of bath toys still out there on the open waves, he started making calculations. He tried to predict where the others would appear. An entire herd of the toys would probably swim right through the Bering Strait together and get stuck in the pack ice. Very slowly, the ice would move eastward, and in about five years they'd likely end up in warmer water near Greenland. The oceanographer offered a reward to anyone who found one of these bath toys in the Atlantic Ocean. He was eventually proved right: ducks, frogs, beavers, and turtles were found in Canada, Iceland, and later even in Ireland and England. Other toys had floated toward Korea, Hawaii, and Australia. There must be thousands of them still bobbing around out there. If you find one, you should drop Curtis Ebbesmeyer a line: CurtisEbbesmeyer@comcast.net.

The rubber duckies and their friends were able to travel so far because of the currents in the oceans. On the surface, the wind provides the current. But in deeper water, it's mainly a result of the differences in salt content and temperature. Warm is lighter than cold, and fresh water is lighter than salt water. So if water is salty or cold, it sinks. If water is fresh or warm, it rises. This creates all kinds of currents in the oceans. Water rises like an escalator, drops like a waterfall, races like a rollercoaster, rushing over and under and through. Where water disappears, new water has to fill the gap. Where water appears, other water has to leave. It's a complicated system in which everything is connected to everything else.

A change in temperature can have serious consequences. You can see this, for example, in the weather phenomenon of El Niño, between South America and Indonesia. Normally, the east wind pushes the warm ocean water from Peru to Indonesia. This creates space off the coast of Peru for cold water from the deep sea. That cold water ensures dry weather. Above warm water, heavy showers develop. But when the east wind drops, the currents turn around. Then the warm water flows to South America. Australia and Indonesia get the dry weather now. Harvests fail and lots of forest fires break out. Along the coast of South America, though, it becomes warmer and wetter. The sudden rain causes mudflows and landslides. But the consequences of El Niño can also be felt elsewhere. Drought causes hunger and famine all the way to southern Africa. An average El Niño lasts around six months before the situation slowly returns to normal.

However, changing currents can have other consequences. Some scientists say that Europe will become a lot colder because of climate change. Huh? Colder because the Earth is warming up? They're talking about the warm Gulf Stream. At the moment, this ensures that winters in Amsterdam and London are much milder than winters in New York and Toronto, even though those cities are much farther south. This is because the ocean current carries warm water from the Gulf of Mexico all the way to northern Europe. Near Greenland, the water cools off. As a result, it occupies less space, becomes heavier, and sinks to the bottom. The cold water flows back along the American coast to the south as an undersea river.

In recent years, the Gulf Stream appears to have been getting a little weaker. This may be because so much ice is melting in Greenland that the fresh meltwater is disturbing the Gulf Stream. The fresh water floats on the salt water and stops the current. If the warm water can no longer reach northern Europe, it could become 10 degrees colder there. It would not be the first time that a big dose of fresh water has disrupted the Gulf Stream. Ten thousand years ago, an American glacial lake emptied and half the world was suddenly plunged into the cold.

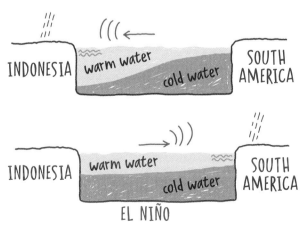

Acid Oceans

Seventy percent of the Earth is covered with water. Scientists don't yet understand half of it. So they've tipped about 4,000 robots overboard from research ships. Scattered throughout the world's seas, they work hard to collect details about the oceans. Every robot is two meters long and looks like a gas cylinder with an antenna on its head. All by themselves, they dive to a depth of one kilometer. For around nine days, they float along on the current. As they go, they measure the temperature and the salt content of the water. Then they descend to a depth of two kilometers. They continue measuring and return to the surface. Using their antenna, they pass on the measurements to satellites—and then they dive back down again.

Thanks to these robots, we know that the oceans have absorbed a lot of CO_2 and a lot of heat in recent years. So much, in fact, that for about 15 years it looked as if the Earth was hardly warming up at all. But now it turns out that the oceans absorbed that heat. In recent years, this has been happening more slowly. It seems as if the oceans are almost full of CO_2 and heat.

CO_2 disappears in the water in various ways. Algae and plankton use it to make oxygen. But CO_2 also partially dissolves in water. This creates carbonic acid, which you know as the fizz in fizzy drinks. This carbonic acid is making the oceans more and more acidic. You can't taste it, but it's

bad news for the coral, the algae, and the plankton. They grow less and so can absorb less and less CO_2. This can be seen in the latest measurements from the robots.

The warming of the water is also a factor, because the warmer the water is, the worse it is at holding on to CO_2. You can test this out for yourself with two cans of soda. Put one can in the refrigerator and one in a warm place. When the first can is nice and cold, open both of the cans. Watch out— if the warm can is very warm, the soda will come frothing out. The warm soda loses its fizz really quickly, while the cold one will fizz away quite happily for some time. Taste it—the cold soda will be much fizzier. That fizz is from the CO_2 in the drink. Cold liquid retains CO_2 much better than warm liquid. This is true for fizzy drinks and for the water of the oceans. In warm oceans, the CO_2 disappears into the atmosphere much more easily.

So the oceans slow down the warming of the Earth by absorbing CO_2 and heat. But in an ocean that's warmer and more acidic, there's less and less room for CO_2. There comes a point when the ocean can't take any more. So more CO_2 remains in the air and the temperature starts to rise more quickly.

Stormy Weather

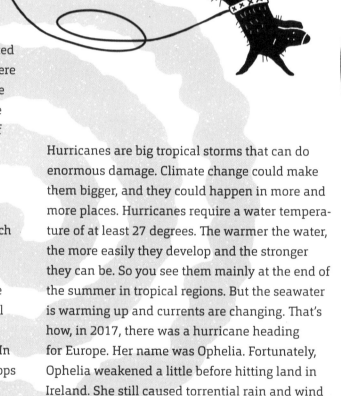

And now the forecast for the coming century. In most places, the temperature will rise by between one and four degrees. Dry regions will become drier, and wet regions will become wetter. The hurricane season will be longer, the hurricanes will be bigger, and they may also turn up in unexpected places. On all continents except Antarctica, there will be a greater chance of heat waves, and the heat waves will last longer. There will be more periods of serious drought, but also periods of heavy rain. Bad weather will involve more powerful gusts of wind, more thunderstorms, and bigger hailstones.

Weather forecasts have to be taken with a pinch of salt. Predicting the climate is even trickier. That's why these predictions are based on the calculations of thousands of computers. These predict, for example, that the drier regions will become drier and the wet ones wetter. This happens because of the higher temperatures. In regions where it is already dry, the last few drops of water will evaporate and so it will become even drier. In regions that are wet, more water will evaporate too. This means that there will be more water in the air, and it will also rain more.

Hurricanes are big tropical storms that can do enormous damage. Climate change could make them bigger, and they could happen in more and more places. Hurricanes require a water temperature of at least 27 degrees. The warmer the water, the more easily they develop and the stronger they can be. So you see them mainly at the end of the summer in tropical regions. But the seawater is warming up and currents are changing. That's how, in 2017, there was a hurricane heading for Europe. Her name was Ophelia. Fortunately, Ophelia weakened a little before hitting land in Ireland. She still caused torrential rain and wind speeds of up to 150 kilometers an hour. The storm resulted in at least five deaths and millions and millions of dollars' worth of damage.

Scientists are still arguing about whether global warming is going to mean more hurricanes or not. But the hurricanes that do happen will probably be stronger on average and, like Ophelia, sometimes happen in strange places.

Hurricanes and other storms can be more violent because warmer air contains more water vapor. This means that the showers that fall are often worse. How does that happen? For water to evaporate, heat is required. This heat is released when the steam turns back into drops of water. This is exactly what happens in clouds. Clouds develop because water vapor cools and drops of water form. As a result, the air inside the cloud warms up and is warmer than the surrounding air: this allows the cloud to keep floating along like a hot-air balloon. With more water vapor in the air, the cloud can become even warmer. That means that it goes higher, just like a hot-air balloon when the balloonist heats the air inside. And the higher the cloud, the more violent the weather.

Inside a cloud, the particles are constantly whizzing past one another. Warm air rises and cold air sinks. The higher the cloud, the faster this happens. It's a sort of vertical wind. Drops of water hitch a ride on these currents of air. The little drops that are formed are not heavy enough to fall. They drift back up and grow when they collide with other drops of water. When they are heavy enough, they finally fall. So warm air produces both higher clouds and heavier showers.

Thunderstorms develop because the drops of water freeze and ice crystals form. When ice crystals rub against one another, they create electric charges, like when you rub a balloon over a woolen sweater. The harder you rub, the more it crackles. In the same way, a bigger electric charge in the clouds creates more serious storms.

Hail also develops because of the air currents in the cloud. Cold drops of water climb into the cloud, where it's even colder, and the drops of water collide with ice crystals. Together, they are heavier and they sink deeper into the cloud. From there, they rise again, growing in size. This continues until the hailstone is too heavy to remain inside the cloud. Then it plummets to the ground at great speed. The higher the clouds are, the longer the hailstones continue to grow. This means that larger hailstones can fall in a warmer climate. And the bigger they are, the harder and faster they fall. A hailstone the size of a tennis ball can easily get up to a speed of 120 kilometers an hour.

And So On

Global warming causes the Earth to warm up even more. That might sound strange, but it's true. It's because of climate amplifiers. You know about these already: the warming makes the ice melt, so the Earth becomes less white and absorbs more heat, and so the ice melts all the more. These kinds of amplifiers play a nasty role in climate change. Here are another two.

Think back to that café you sat outside with your mom and dad on that hot day on your vacation. Was it last year or the year before? Doesn't matter. Your mom and dad asked: "What do you want to drink?" "Soda! Now!" As soon as the waiter brought the order, you grabbed the bottle. Want to bet that the bottle was already completely wet at that point? And that there was soon a puddle of water on the table where the bottle had been? That water comes from the air. It's invisible water vapor that's all around us. As soon as it gets cold—on a cool bottle, for example—the water vapor transforms into drops.

There's usually more water vapor in warm air than in cold air. This is why you see that puddle of water on the table more often in the summer than in the winter. And it's why water vapor is also a kind of climate amplifier. Water vapor holds on to heat, just like CO_2 and methane. When it's warmer, more water evaporates and there's more water vapor to hold on to the heat. That makes it even warmer, and even more water vapor ends up in the air, which also holds on to more heat. And so on and so on.

For another climate amplifier, we should visit the outdoor freezer in Russia. Two researchers, both wrapped up warm, are walking across a frozen lake in Siberia, in the east of the country. Bubbles of various sizes can be seen in the ice. Using a metal bar, one of the researchers cuts into a bubble. The other holds up a lighter and... whoosh! A flame of at least a meter in height shoots up into the air. They know that it's methane. This develops when bacteria feed on the remains of dead plants and animals. There are plenty of these in the ground here.

The ground has been frozen for at least 100,000 years. The people who live in this region have a hard life. The top layer of earth melts very briefly, only in the summer. Plants and animals that die are frozen as soon as the long winter returns. Just like peat, they're preserved well because there is not much oxygen. That means they don't get the chance to start rotting. This has been going on for many thousands of years, and millions of animals and plants are lying safely here in the ice, like fish sticks and spinach in the freezer. But when you turn off the freezer, the food starts to rot. Bacteria seize their chance and leave behind nasty smells. That's what happens in Siberia too.

The frozen soil thaws. The melted ice creates swamps and lakes. In the soil, the bacteria have a nibble of the defrosting mammoths and reindeer. And, as you know, where there's oxygen around, CO_2 develops. Without oxygen, methane remains. The gases escape upward. The water of the lake blows bubbles like a Jacuzzi. In the winter, these bubbles end up in the ice. When the ice melts or when someone makes a hole in the ice, the gases disappear into the atmosphere.

This thawing of the ground does not only take place in Siberia. In total, an area twice the size of Europe is frozen. There's a huge supply of carbon in the soil—more than four times as much as combined in all the plants and trees that are now alive. Almost half of that frozen ground is on the point of thawing. This does not happen suddenly, but gradually. Methane and CO_2 are released into the air, and they heat up the Earth even more, which causes even more ice to thaw, so that more methane and CO_2 are released into the air. And so on and so on. So that's a real climate amplifier too.

On the Brink

Some moments can change your life. A high note that you sing at an audition, a car that almost knocks you down, a brave text message that you send—or don't send—to that person you like in your class. Moments like that are called tipping points. The Earth has them too. And, as in the examples above, some tipping points are a lot more serious than others.

URK

We call something a tipping point when there has been a change—and there's no going back. Like the last dodo dropping dead. With climate change, that usually means that the climate amplifiers can no longer be stopped. The end of the warm Gulf Stream could be such a point. It's hard to predict if and when it will happen. But if it does happen, we'll have only ourselves to blame and there will be no way to reverse it.

You've already read that the ice cap of Greenland could melt completely too. That's not a certainty. It depends on the temperature, on climate amplifiers, and also on a lot of other things, such as the influence of moulins and cryoconite. If the melting suddenly speeds up to the point where all these things reinforce one another, there'll be no turning back. And there we'll be, with a seven-meter rise in the sea level.

The methane released from the thawing soil is sometimes seen as a tipping point too. However, this happens quite gradually, and it's not the time bomb that people sometimes see it as. Some say there's a time bomb at the bottom of the sea though. The low temperatures are keeping huge amounts of methane down there. There's more energy than in all the natural gas, oil, and coal on Earth combined. If the seawater and the bottom of the sea warm up, the methane could thaw and find its way out. Then we'll have a sudden and long heat wave, like with the farts from the sea 55 million years ago.

METHANE

The Amazon, the biggest rainforest in the world, could also hit a tipping point. Climate change generally makes wet regions wetter, but in the Amazon it's actually becoming dry more often. The warming up of the oceans changes the air currents, so there's less rainfall above land. The constant deforestation doesn't help either. Trees absorb water, but then most of the moisture evaporates through their leaves. So fewer trees result in less evaporation. The rainy season is getting shorter and shorter and the temperatures are higher and higher, so the forest has less and less time to flourish again. If the forest disappears, lots of carbon will be released into the air and even less rain will fall. Scientists are carrying out research and using computer models to try to predict where this is all going. Some of them say that the Amazon rainforest could change into desert within half a century. You can see why people are afraid of such tipping points. They're hard to predict and they often have a huge impact. Disaster movies and fantasy novels put them to good use. They like to scare us with the idea of a scorched Earth, flooded cities, or climate wars. But will it really come to that?

6 Calamity & Disaster

In which you will read... why there's a flag at the bottom of the Arctic Ocean • which islands are at risk of going glug • why Sandy wasn't welcome in New York • how your smartphone is making people thirsty in Bolivia • why Brussels will never break the world record for rain • what the world's most dangerous animal is doing in the Netherlands • what to do with your grandma and grandpa in a heat wave • how weather experts can save chocolate • why there's not a book about water wars.

In short: about the consequences of the consequences of climate change.

The Good News

I have good news and I have bad news. The bad news is that there isn't that much good news when it comes to climate change. So let's just begin with the bit of good news that we do have.

Climate change isn't much of a problem for the Earth. It's mainly a problem for us people and the other living creatures on the planet. Earth has already been through so many climate changes. It'll survive this one too. When there are no more people around to cut down forests, the excess of CO_2 will naturally be taken out of the air by the trees. The climate will recover, and another species will probably come along that can rule the roost on Earth.

CO_2 is good for trees and other plants. And so it's good for agriculture. Hurrah! Plants use CO_2 to grow. So more CO_2 results in more growth. Some farmers also make use of CO_2 to make their plants grow better. It's too bad that CO_2 has so many disadvantages, as you can read on just about every other page of this book.

And there's more good news. Lots of people are happy about higher temperatures. This is particularly true in places where it's a bit chilly now. Colder countries are moving toward a warmer climate now too, which means people from places like Canada won't have to travel so far to find good weather during their vacations. Nice! And in countries where it's really cold now, a warmer climate could even save lives, as sometimes it's so cold that people die.

Many regions that are now frozen will thaw. This has a positive side too. For example, more Greenlanders are starting to grow fruit and vegetables, and they are able to take more valuable rocks and metals from the ground that is emerging from under the ice. Fishers are happy with the mackerel and other fish that are slowly making their way closer to the north.

Half of the world is rubbing its hands at the thought of the North Pole region thawing. Russia, Norway, Denmark, Canada, and the United States are all keen to annex as much of the area as possible. In 2007, a Russian submarine even ventured to the bottom of the Arctic Ocean to plant a

+ GOOD NEWS + CLIMATE CHANGE NOT A PROBLEM FOR THE EARTH
EXTRA INCOME FOR GREENLAND + NORTH POLE FULL OF RESOURC

was given the name Ötzi, after the valley where he was found, the Ötztal. The body was well preserved. Together with his clothes, weapons, and tools, Ötzi provided a lot of information about the Stone Age. Archeologists expect that a lot more old remains will emerge from beneath the ice.

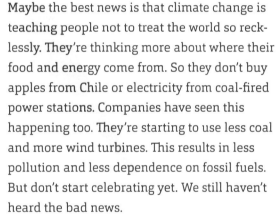

Russian flag there. The North Pole is so much in demand because there is less and less ice now. That means that ships can make increasing use of this route to sail from Europe to Japan and China. It's a lot shorter than the normal route through the Suez Canal in Egypt. But what's even more important is the oil and natural gas that must be in the ground there. It's worth billions.

Maybe the best news is that climate change is teaching people not to treat the world so recklessly. They're thinking more about where their food and energy come from. So they don't buy apples from Chile or electricity from coal-fired power stations. Companies have seen this happening too. They're starting to use less coal and more wind turbines. This results in less pollution and less dependence on fossil fuels. But don't start celebrating yet. We still haven't heard the bad news.

The thawing of the ice and earth is also increasingly exposing our history. More and more mammoths are coming out of the deep-frozen Russian soil. This is fascinating for scientists. In 1991, two mountaineers in the Alps found a man who must have died there 5,300 years ago. The ice mummy

Ötzi the Iceman
+/- 3300 CE
+/- 3255 CE

GOOD FOR TREES AND PLANTS + NICE AND WARM +
MORE AND MORE MAMMOTHS AND MUMMIES + PEOPLE THINK

Disappearing Islands

Did you have plans for a vacation in Kiribati? Maybe it's a bit far, but it's beautiful. White beaches, blue sea, and palm trees—that kind of thing. Kiribati is in the Pacific Ocean, to the east of Australia. It's made up entirely of tropical islands and sea. Very small islands. So small that on the world map they can easily hide behind the dots on the *i*'s of *Kiribati*.

But anyway, if you're planning on heading there, I wouldn't wait too long. The rising water level is making the islands smaller and smaller. The rise isn't happening very quickly, only a few millimeters a year at most. But whenever there's a storm, the sea eats away another piece of the tropical paradise. And there are more extreme storms now, because of global warming. The president of Kiribati has already bought some land for his citizens on the neighboring Fiji Islands. At least they have mountains there. That's not the case in Kiribati. Those islands are just a couple of meters above sea level. So the inhabitants are scared that they will soon disappear under water.

According to predictions, that will happen in this century. The inhabitants have come up with all kinds of ideas to prevent it. Raising the islands, putting a barrier around them, constructing floating islands… But it's all too expensive or impractical. The people of Kiribati are already having problems because of the seawater. The coast is crumbling away. The salt water is ruining their crops. Some islanders are moving to New

Zealand and Australia. They have been called the first climate refugees, but that's a bit of an exaggeration. Climate refugees are people who have to leave their home because of drought, flooding, or extreme weather. Most of the Kiribati migrants are simply going in search of a better life. But it's only a matter of time before the inhabitants of these islands have to escape from the water. The same is true for other tropical islands, such as Nauru, Tuvalu, and the Maldives.

However, 8,000 kilometers to the north, the people are perhaps even worse off. The houses of Shishmaref really are on the brink of disaster. Just one storm and the sea could sweep them away. Shishmaref is a village with fewer than 600 inhabitants. It's situated on a long island in Alaska. There are no bikinis, flip-flops, or hammocks there. The Inuit wear hats, boots, and warm coats. They catch fish and hunt seals and reindeer. But that's becoming increasingly difficult. The higher temperatures mean that there is less ice—and that the ice is not entirely to be trusted. If they're not careful, hunters can sink through the ice on their snowmobiles or fall into a hole.

Most of the houses in Shishmaref are close to the sea. That hasn't always been the case. In the past, there was a wide beach between the houses and the sea, and the ground was frozen all year long. The waves didn't stand a chance. In the fall, there was ice along the coast, which protected the people from storms. But now the waves and the wind are free to do their thing. More and more of the coast of Shishmaref is crumbling away. The inhabitants are leaving their homes to start new lives elsewhere, farther inland. The empty houses are balancing on the brink. Some are still standing straight, but the ground beneath them has been swept away. Others are already tilting and are waiting for the sea to make the final push.

A few years ago, the inhabitants of Shishmaref voted to move to a safer place, 80 kilometers away. That's not an easy decision to make. The older inhabitants, in particular, wanted to stay. For now, they're getting their way, as it will cost far too much to move all the residents.

SHISHMAREF

Cities under Threat

New York, October 30, 2012. People are walking the streets with flashlights. Windows have been boarded up. Someone has written GO HOME, SANDY! on the wood in black spray paint. Piles of sandbags are stacked up against doors. The buildings are in darkness. In the distance, you can see light in a neighborhood where the electricity is still working. Traffic lights are black and are swaying in the wind. There are hardly any cars on the streets, just the occasional fire truck or ambulance with wailing sirens. Retailers have closed their shutters. There's not much to buy anyway. Days ago, people started hoarding. Bottles of water, batteries, canned food. No one knew how hard Sandy would hit. But now they do.

Big streets changed into rivers. A construction crane on a skyscraper snapped in the wind. The fronts have been torn off buildings. An amusement park disappeared into the waves. The subway tunnels filled with water. In total, Hurricane Sandy killed 53 people in New York. Hundreds of houses and a quarter of a million cars were damaged. The damage was around $30 billion. And that was just in New York. On the way from Jamaica to Canada, Sandy caused even more death and destruction.

Is that climate change? Hmm, well… We can't be certain, but it looks a lot like it. Warmer air contains more energy and more water. That gave Sandy plenty to work with. Normally a hurricane has weakened to a rainstorm by the time it gets anywhere near New York. A hurricane needs warm water, which is not usually to be found there. But in the fall of 2012, it was.

However, you could identify other causes for Hurricane Sandy. But even if Sandy had nothing to do with global warming, it's still a good example of what's in store for us. Floods. Lots more of them. This is partly to do with rising sea levels. But it's mainly because there are more severe storms. And during a storm the water rises by meters instead of centimeters.

All over the world, cities by the sea are having to deal with more floods. And cities are, of course, exactly where lots and lots of people live and work. How about Rio de Janeiro? Miami, London, Lagos, Istanbul, Dubai, Mumbai, Hong Kong, Jakarta, Tokyo, Sydney? If you add up the inhabitants of those cities, the number comes to more than 100 million. And every day their numbers are growing. There are more houses, roads, pavement. That means more and more places where the water can't just sink into the ground. That really doesn't help when your city floods.

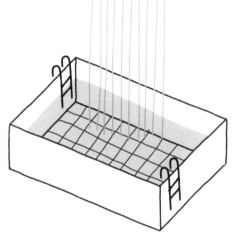

The threat isn't only from the sea. Lots of big cities developed on the banks of a river. Human beings have forced those rivers into a straitjacket. You can flow here—and that's it! But more and more snow is melting and there are more severe storms, so the water in the rivers often rises higher too. Every year, you can see pictures on the news of the Mississippi, the Mekong, or the Thames flooding streets and fields.

New York is also on a river, as are most major coastal cities. New York is on the estuary of the Hudson River. An estuary is the shape of a funnel. When Sandy sent all that water pouring into the funnel, the river quickly rose. Try filling a bottle with a wide bottom and a narrow neck. That's a kind of funnel too. As long as the water is in the wide part, it rises slowly. But as soon as it reaches the neck, everything starts happening a lot faster and you have to turn off the faucet or the bottle will overflow.

Cities like New York are preparing for a future with more high water. To combat the sea, they are building defenses that can be closed temporarily to stop the water entering the river. They fight rising river water with higher dikes or by creating more room in the river. But what happens if the river water is already high and the sea defenses have to close because of a big storm? Then the seawater can't go into the river, and the river water can't go into the sea either. While up in the mountains, the glaciers are melting. Like a faucet you can't turn off. Should the sea defenses be closed or not? You decide.

We Want Water

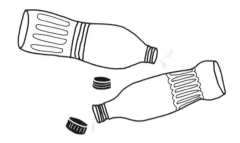

After Lake Titicaca, Lake Poopó is the biggest lake in Bolivia. And the lake with the funniest name, of course. But since 2015, Lake Poopó has no longer been a lake. High temperatures have caused the shallow water to evaporate. Thousands of dead fish lie on the cracked bottom, roasting in the sun. Scattered across the dry plain, fishing boats wait to go sailing again. That moment may never come. The water of Lake Poopó came from rain and from glaciers. But not much rain has fallen in recent years. And less and less is coming from the glaciers because they are getting smaller. However, it's not all the fault of climate change. Farmers and mines in the region secretly took far too much water for themselves. They need the water for agriculture and to get lithium out of the ground, for the battery in your smartphone. The truth is that there's simply not enough water in Bolivia.

Imagine turning on the faucet and nothing coming out. Or flushing the toilet and it doesn't flush. Or going to the store for bottles of water, but the shelves are empty. That was what happened for weeks in large areas of Bolivia. Schools closed their doors. You weren't allowed to go to the

bathroom in restaurants. The government brought in tankers of water, and the people lined up with buckets and basins. They were only given water to drink, not to wash themselves. There wasn't enough for that.

The Bolivians were furious with the government. Carrying empty buckets and bottles, they went out onto the streets to protest. They held up signs saying WE WANT WATER! As if the government could do anything about the fact that there was no water coming out of the faucets. Well, they kind of could. They should have known for a long time that less and less water would be available. Which was a very good reason to use it carefully. By making sure that farmers didn't waste it on their land and that miners didn't take it secretly. And, as in the Amazon, endlessly chopping down trees wasn't a good idea here either.

Bolivia isn't the only country struggling with increasing drought. In the United States, water in California is regularly rationed because there's not enough of it. When rationing happens, it means that people aren't allowed to wash their cars, fill their swimming pools, or spray their golf courses. So it's more of a luxury issue. But drought and storms also cause big forest fires, in California and in other places. And that's not about luxury. People regularly have to flee, and there are deaths and casualties.

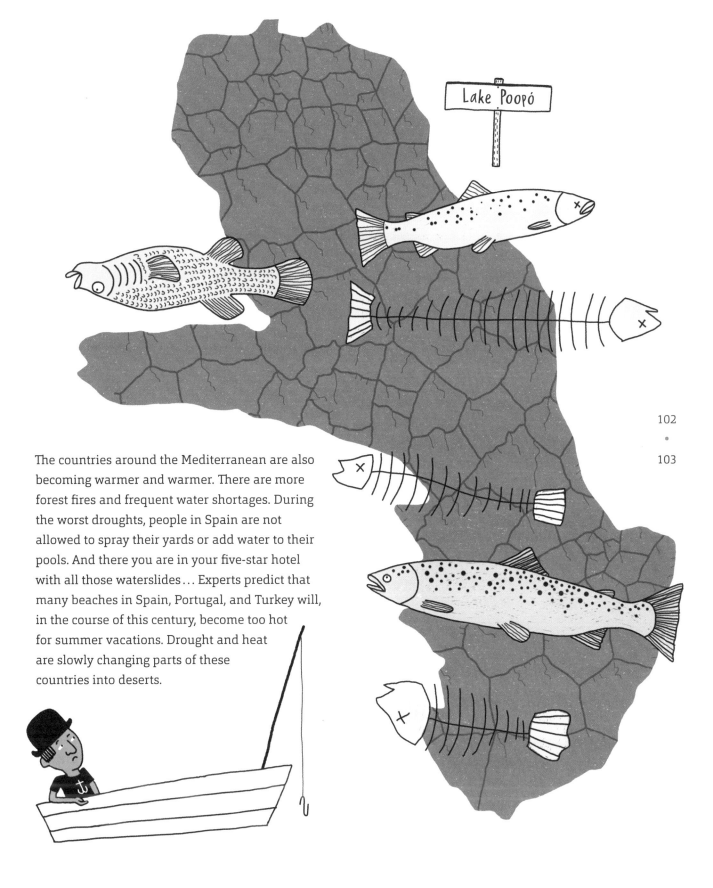

The countries around the Mediterranean are also becoming warmer and warmer. There are more forest fires and frequent water shortages. During the worst droughts, people in Spain are not allowed to spray their yards or add water to their pools. And there you are in your five-star hotel with all those waterslides... Experts predict that many beaches in Spain, Portugal, and Turkey will, in the course of this century, become too hot for summer vacations. Drought and heat are slowly changing parts of these countries into deserts.

Lake Poopó

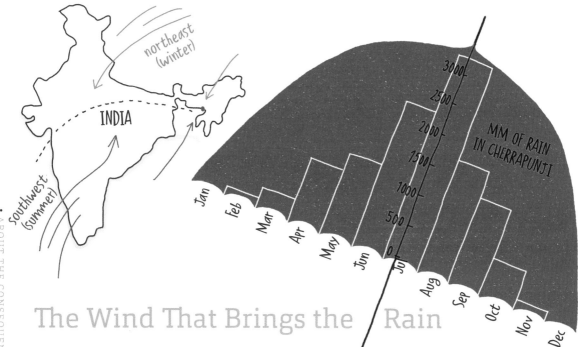

The Wind That Brings the Rain

In the Indian city of Cherrapunji, there is a sign saying THE WETTEST PLACE ON PLANET EARTH. There are places in the world that think they're even wetter, but it's safe to say that Cherrapunji is a wet place. On average, 11 meters of rain fall there every year. That's enough to give a diplodocus a dunking. Compare it to Chicago, where there are around 90 centimeters of rainfall a year, or even rainy Vancouver, which gets roughly 130 centimeters. But it's not always wet in Cherrapunji. In December and January, a couple of centimeters fall at most, while in the summer it pours and pours. The month of July 1861 even made it into the *Guinness Book of Records*. A total of 9.3 meters of rain fell—in a single month.

The big differences in rainfall are because of the monsoon that blows in India and southeast Asia. The monsoon is a wind that first blows one way for six months and then reverses and goes the other way. This has to do with the temperature differences between land and sea. When the wind comes off the land, the air is very dry. When the wind blows from the sea, it brings a huge amount of water with it. Global warming is making these differences even larger. And the monsoon is becoming more difficult to predict. Sometimes it can be very dry and sometimes very wet. Sometimes the monsoon is much too early and sometimes much too late.

That has serious consequences for the inhabitants of this region. There are easily a billion of them. Many of these people depend on the monsoon. Farmers need the rain to grow rice and other crops. If the harvest fails, they don't make any money and there's a risk of famine. But if too much rain falls, the rivers flood. You've probably seen the pictures: the tops of palm trees poking

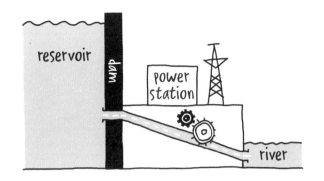

out of the water, houses collapsing into rivers with a crash, fully loaded scooters driving through the brown water. It's all the fault of the monsoon. But the local people can't live without it. You should see what happens when the monsoon is late.

In New Delhi, the temperature goes up to 45 degrees. At night, it's at most a few degrees cooler. The 20 million inhabitants long for cool air. Their fans and air-conditioning are no good to them because the electricity keeps failing. In dozens of cities, people are threatening employees of the electricity companies. They're furious that there's no electricity when they really need it. But that's no coincidence. If everyone turns the air-conditioning all the way up, the power stations have to work at full power. Water is needed for that too. Cooling water for the coal-fired power stations. And lots of water for the hydroelectric power stations. But if the monsoon doesn't show up, the reservoirs will be empty.

Then, almost two weeks later than usual, the rain finally arrives. The children dance in the streets. The dust disappears from the air. The temperature drops from hot to warm. A sigh of relief passes through the city. But along with the water come the mosquitos. And mosquitos bring nasty diseases.

Ticks, Mosquitos, and Pollen

The last outbreak of anthrax in Russia had been in 1941. Anthrax is a pretty contagious disease and, if you're not careful, it can be fatal. And in 2016, the disease suddenly reappeared. Dozens of shepherds from the north of the country ended up in the hospital. A 12-year-old boy died. They had probably been infected by bacteria in the thawing carcass of a reindeer.

The animal must have died of anthrax at least 75 years ago. Its dead body froze and the bacteria inside it ended up in a kind of stasis. Now that the ground in that area is thawing, the bacteria are coming back to life. The anthrax bacteria will wake up in other places in northern Russia too. But anthrax is probably the only disease that can last for so long in ice. Luckily, there is a vaccine that helps against the disease. So there's no need to be afraid of it.

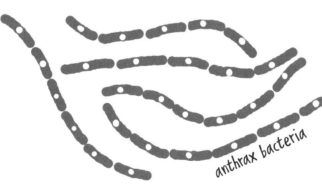

anthrax bacteria

What you do need to be afraid of, though, is ticks. Little spider-like creatures that can transmit Lyme disease. You might already know that. But did you know that ticks are over the moon about global warming? Just think about it. They love heat and humidity. Check! They're active when it's warmer than five degrees. Check! And they like to hitch a ride on people who go into forests, countryside, and dunes. Who are in those places when it's warm. Check! So it's no wonder that there are more and more ticks, that the ticks are active for longer, and that your camp counselors keep nagging you to do a tick check when you come in after a day outside.

Mosquitos really love climate change too. Take the malaria mosquito. It's the most dangerous creature on the planet: every year, half a million people die of the disease that it transmits. That's a bit more than the 150,000 people a year who are killed by venomous snakes. Malaria mosquitos love heat and humidity. So the future is looking good for them. To the north and south of the tropics, the climate is becoming better and better for the mosquito. And mountains where it was once too cold for them are also coming within their reach. This will result in a lot more victims, particularly in Africa.

tick

In wealthy regions, people don't need to be so afraid of malaria. Even if they get tropical conditions, there are far fewer dirty pools of water for the mosquitos there, and there's much more money to combat them. But the cousins and various other relatives of the mosquito are on the move as well. The tiger mosquito and the Asian bush mosquito can transmit diseases such as dengue fever. They hitch a ride to other countries in bamboo and car tires that have a bit of water left in them. In order to transmit a disease, they must be able to reproduce and be infected with the disease. That chance is still very small.

One really obvious sign of climate change is all the sniffing and sneezing around you. Maybe you join in, like I do. In the past, I used to have hay fever for a couple of weeks in May, when everything was in bloom where I live. But now I sometimes find myself sneezing from March to October. That's because the warm weather is making some plants flower much earlier. And when one has just finished flowering, another starts tossing its pollen into the air. Because of the higher temperatures, plants also seem to be spreading much more pollen. And then there are all those plants from the south, which used to think it was too cold here. So if someone says climate change is nonsense, then I just say, "Achoo!"

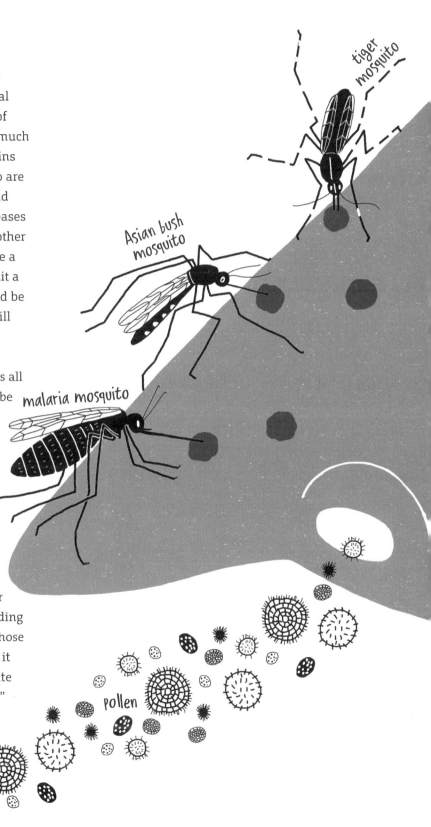

tiger mosquito

Asian bush mosquito

malaria mosquito

Pollen

Spoilsports

August 18, 2011. In the Belgian town of Hasselt, the Pukkelpop music festival is in full swing. In the blazing sun, the temperature gets up to 28 degrees. There's a forecast of stormy weather, but no one is worried. Wearing shorts and light T-shirts, thousands of people are watching their favorite bands. Then suddenly the sky turns dark. The rain pours and the wind howls. Big hailstones fall from the sky. In panic, the festivalgoers run into tents, which collapse under the force of the wind and the rain. Five people die that day. The rest of the festival is canceled.

October 12, 2018. At Desert Daze in southern California, Tame Impala is playing their first song. The light show, however, is being taken over by nature. Lightning strikes all around the festival area. After 15 minutes the band leaves the stage. Threatening clouds are rolling in, and event organizers issue a warning: "Due to safety concerns regarding dangerous weather, we are asking all guests to immediately exit the Desert Daze grounds and return to their cars and seek shelter. We ask that you stay in your cars and remain calm."

With anxious faces, the festivalgoers do as they've been told. The grass turns into mud, but fortunately no one is injured.

Was the bad weather at these music festivals the fault of climate change? We can't tell for certain. Storms like that happened long before the invention of the steam engine too. There are also a lot more people now—and a lot more festivals. But storms do happen more often because of climate change. As you'll notice when sports matches and games are cancelled more often. Or festivals or other outdoor events. No one wants to get struck by lightning or hit by a massive hailstone.

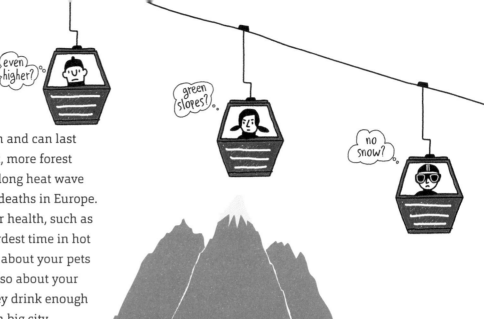

Heat waves also occur more often and can last longer. This means more drought, more forest fires, and more deaths. During a long heat wave in 2003, there were 70,000 extra deaths in Europe. Most of these were people in poor health, such as elderly people. They have the hardest time in hot temperatures. So don't just think about your pets during the next heat wave, but also about your grandparents. Make sure that they drink enough water. Particularly if they live in a big city.

In a big city, it can easily be five degrees hotter than outside the city. How is that possible? Try feeling a wall that the sun has been shining on. It'll stay warm for hours. So the buildings in a city hold on to a lot of heat. The dark color of the plazas and roads also make the city absorb more heat. Less wind develops between the buildings to cool things down. People add a degree or two with their cars, air-conditioning, and their bodies at 37 degrees. And in most cities there's not much water and not much greenery, which can create a cooling effect through evaporation. So if you're the mayor of a big city, now you know how to prepare your city for climate change: make sure there's more shade, more wind, more greenery, more water, and less traffic—and paint all the roofs and roads white.

Speaking of white, do you have any plans to go on a winter vacation? Then you really shouldn't leave it much longer. Because the winters are getting warmer too. And so there's less snow falling in the

mountains. Every year, millions of people travel to the Rocky Mountains and the Alps for a bit of winter skiing. The season for skiing and other snow sports is getting shorter, though—and that's no fun. But the winter sports fans themselves have contributed to global warming, with those energy-guzzling snow-making machines, the traffic jams on the way to the resorts, and all those trees that were cut down to make places to ski. So the snow arrives later and later and it doesn't hang around for as long. Anyone who wants to ski or snowboard properly has to go higher into the mountains. Some scientists studying the Alps in Europe predict that there won't be any ski lifts left there by the end of the century—unless they leave a few for lazy alpine hikers.

Food for Everyone

For just a dollar, you can buy a Snickers bar, a bag of M&Ms, or a soft-serve ice-cream cone from a fast-food restaurant. If you think about it, that's incredible. Particularly when you know everything that goes into making chocolate. Cocoa beans for certain. They grow on the cocoa tree, of course. And cocoa trees are found mainly in countries around the equator. There's a reason for that. They want to be warm, but not hot. They can't stand drought, but they don't like too much water either. They're actually big old whiners. And so the changing climate could cause problems for them. The people who make all those tasty chocolate bars are aware of this. They've even employed weather experts to research how they can make sure that the cocoa trees will continue to produce enough in the future. That's not just important for them and for the cocoa farmers, but also for chocolate lovers. Imagine if the shelves were empty or if a Snickers bar cost five dollars. That could happen. In the past, chocolate was just for the rich.

But hey, there are worse things. Famine, for example, and malnutrition. So let's first make sure that the world's population has enough to eat. Then you're talking mainly about rice, corn, and wheat. Those plants are a bit less fussy than cocoa beans. But they're not keen on drought, floods, storms, hail, and plagues of insects either. And—wouldn't you know it?—those are the consequences of climate change that you've just been reading about. So you can see why some people are afraid that there soon won't be enough food for everyone, particularly when the world's population just keeps on growing.

The crops won't suffer everywhere though. Lots of areas that for a long time were too cold to grow certain foods are becoming increasingly suitable. Canada, for example, or Greenland, Scandinavia, and northern Russia. In Africa, farmers are going to have to look in higher places for cooler weather. The mountains of Ethiopia and Tanzania, for instance. But generally Africa is going to have a hard time of it, also because this is the continent where the population is growing fastest. More and more people are coming along, but it's becoming harder to grow food in many places. And that's just the vegetables and grain we're talking about, not the fish. Lots of fish in the oceans also think it's becoming too hot. They're heading for cooler

Cocoa bean

Cocoa bean CHOCOLATE

Cocoa bean

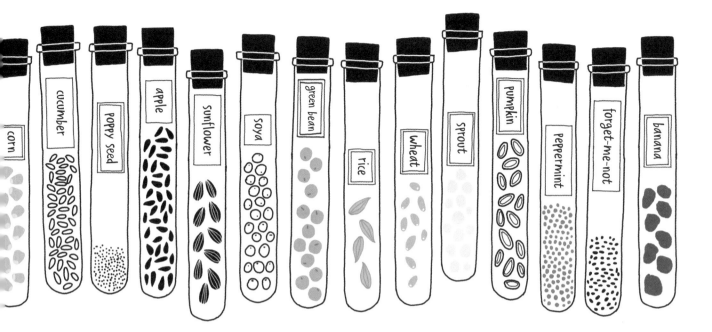

water and swimming to the north and the south. Away from the equator, away from Africa, where lots of people really need the fish in order to get enough nutrition.

While the population is growing and the Earth is becoming warmer, scientists all over the world are working hard to make varieties of grain that are better at withstanding heat, disease, drought, and floods. They do this by crossing varieties, and also by changing the properties of plants in their laboratories. To do this, they use the strengths of different types of seeds. Many countries have their own seedbanks where they safely store all the seeds of that country.

On the Norwegian island of Spitsbergen, there's even a world seedbank, the Global Seed Vault. This is a sort of Noah's ark for plants. In an underground safe, already more than a million sorts of seeds are stored (in total, 2.5 billion seeds can be stored here), just in case they are ever

lost—for example, because of disease, war, or natural disaster. This is particularly important for plants that are often eaten, such as rice, wheat, and beans. Imagine if one of those species died out! So it's good to know that you can make a fresh start. Spitsbergen was chosen as the location for the vault because there are never any wars or earthquakes in this region. The ground is deep-frozen, so the seeds will remain fresh for hundreds of years, even if the freezer breaks down. The builders have also taken the rising sea levels into account: the building is deep inside a hill at a height of 130 meters. Even if all the ice in the world melts, the vault will remain above water.

Water Fights

Now things are going to get really scary. At least, that was my plan. With countries that have to fight for water or shade as a result of climate change. A kind of real-life Hunger Games. The title of this section was going to be Water War or Climate War. Which sounds exciting enough. It was going to start with the fight for a dam. Because rivers don't recognize borders. Anyone who builds a dam just before their border is going to make their neighboring country mad. And the worse the drought, the madder the neighbor will be. As it gets warmer, there would be more wars. Rich people would retreat high into the mountains. Where it's still kind of cool and where a little rain still falls. Where they can easily resist attacks from climate refugees who have had to leave their dry countries behind. There would not be enough water or enough space to allow all the inhabitants of Earth to live. After a while, the 21st century would be no more than a memory of the most prosperous era of humankind. "Do you remember? Back then we used to worry about selfies instead of a cup of clean water." And unlike in a disaster movie, there wouldn't be any hero coming to save us.

But there's no proof at all that this is what's going to happen. In the last 30 years, the number of wars has in fact halved—while the world has become warmer. A few years ago, the author Wendy Barnaby wanted to write a book about water wars. She also liked a bit of scary stuff. Her publisher thought it sounded like a good plan, because everyone believed that in a warmer world there would be more and more fights for water. Barnaby went in search of previous arguments about water. And what did she find? Thousands of dams have been built in rivers without it causing wars. All of the disputes were settled by govern-

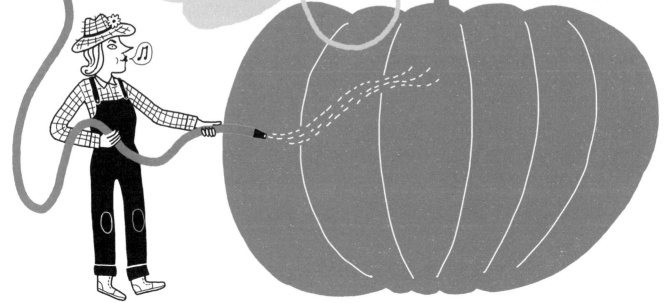

ments. Countries don't want to fight about water at all. Most water is needed to grow food. If you don't have enough water yourself, you simply buy your food in another country. If you have enough money, of course. So the book about water wars was never written.

However, there are some people who believe that climate change will lead to war. Some think the first climate wars are already taking place. They say that the wars in Sudan and Syria are a result of drought. When there was enough to eat and drink, people lived together in peace. Because of the drought, they're now fighting for water, food, and fertile soil. Others say it would never have come to violence if the population groups did not think so differently. The groups that are fighting have different religions or different opinions, and the changes in the climate have simply given them more to argue about.

So it's hard to say if climate change will cause that many wars. It's perhaps even more difficult to predict the number of climate refugees. According to the United Nations, 150 million climate refugees are already on the move, and by 2050 it will be 300 million. That's 300 times the number that crossed the Mediterranean in rickety boats in 2015—and even that was hard for Europe to handle.

Just as with war, it's hard to say if the climate is really the reason for people becoming refugees. Take a poor family living on the coast of Bangla-desh who can barely keep their heads above water. Yet another flood could be the final straw for them. So are they fleeing because of poverty or because of the water? Either way, it's a miserable situation. No one would choose to leave their home and country under normal circumstances.

The crazy thing is that it's mainly poor countries and poor people that suffer because of the consequences of climate change, even though they've emitted much less CO_2 than the wealthy countries. Lots of poor countries are in regions where it's already warm and dry. A couple of degrees more is much worse in those places than in rich countries, which are often cooler. Rich countries also have much more money to build dams, for instance, or to combat disease or buy extra grain. It's no wonder that climate refugees want to go there.

7 Pika & Cephalopod

In which you will read... about the cutest animal you've never heard of • about the bird who thinks the world isn't big enough • who wouldn't mind if the polar bear became extinct • how a tree can save lives • what extinction looks like • why climate change can give you the creeps • how to make a shell vanish.

In short: about the consequences for nature.

Pika Boo, I See You!

Li Weidong
conservationist

Li Weidong was 28 when he saw the animal for the first time, high in the mountains of China. He'd just sat down to rest from a long climb. Suddenly a shadow flashed past. Li looked at the spot where the creature had vanished and could hardly believe his eyes. From between the rocks, a creature from a fairy tale was peeping out at him. It looked a bit like a rabbit, but smaller and with shorter ears. And cuter, much cuter. He'd never seen an animal like that before. Maybe no one had ever seen an animal like that before.

Li Weidong decided to do some research into this new species. The animal belonged to the pika family—that much was clear. Pikas are nicknamed "whistling hares" because they whistle to warn one another of danger. There are different sorts of pika in Asia and America. But none of them looked like the pikas in the Ili region. Li called this species the Ili pika. After that first time, he hardly ever saw any pikas there again. He did find traces though and calculated that there must be around 3,000 Ili pikas living in the area.

Li went on searching. Year after year after year. For 24 years, he didn't see a single one. Until 2014, when another cute little face popped up between the rocks. Li even managed to take a couple of photographs. Just google "Ili pika" and the photos will be at the top of the page. Underneath, you'll see animals that look like him. Those are the other pikas. Distant cousins from the mountains of American and Asia. If you look down the

Google page, you'll even find pictures of Pikachu, the famous Pokémon.

Things are not going well for pikas. Not in Asia and not in America. At this moment, there are only a thousand, at most, of the 3,000 Ili pikas left. Pikas are worse at handling the heat than your grandma is. A few hours spent in temperatures above 26 degrees can mean their death. Global warming has forced the pikas higher and higher into the mountains, which are like islands of coolness in a sea of heat. But the heat is rising too, and the islands are getting smaller. Valleys where it was once cold enough to cross or to go looking for food are now desperately dangerous.

· ABOUT THE CONSEQUENCES FOR NATURE ·

As a result, the pikas are finding it more and more difficult to track down enough food and nice pika partners.

Pikas are not the only animals who are moving house because of climate change. The Americans Camille Parmesan and Gary Yohe have examined thousands of books and notes written by nature lovers. People who—year in, year out— noted when and where they saw certain animals or flowers. Until 1950, they didn't find much shocking in those figures. But after that point they saw a clear development. On average, plant and animal species are moving 600 meters toward the poles every year. And 60 centimeters up into the mountains.

All these relocations could cause problems. Because not everyone moves at the same speed. People who live in a new residential area some-times complain that there aren't any stores there yet. It's the same for some animals. When they've just relocated, there isn't any food for them. In nature, everything is connected. At school, they call this the food chain, the food pyramid, or the food web. If you take away one link in the chain, it causes problems for the others. This also happens because of the changes in the seasons. Plants are starting to bloom earlier. So lots of animals are having to adjust their schedule. Insects are attracted by the flowers. The insects are food for the birds. Those birds are prey for birds of prey and for foxes. Ultimately, they all depend on the plants.

And how are things going to turn out for the whistling hares? Li Weidong is afraid that they're going to become extinct. They have to keep moving higher to escape the heat. When they reach the top of the mountain, there will be nowhere left for them to go. It's too bad they're not in touch with their family in the United States. A group of pikas there has found a different approach. They've gone down into a cool valley instead. Okay, they have to eat different plants, but it looks like they're going to make it.

Adapt, relocate, or die out: for many animals and plants, those are the three choices. Lots of species were already doing this, but because of climate change it's happening all over now. In the air, at the poles, in the jungle, in the desert, on the streets, and in the ocean.

60 cm ↕

Camille Parmesan
biologist

Gary Yohe
economist

Meet the Bee-Eater

People in Amsterdam and Brussels are used to lovely though dull-looking birds like sparrows and pigeons. But now there's something new. It has a bright green-blue belly, an orange-brown back and head, a yellow chin and cheeks, and a cool black mask from its beak to over its eyes. May I introduce you to… the bee-eater? I'll give you three guesses what it eats. It catches the bees in the air and bashes them against a branch to remove the sting. Mmm, tasty! The bee-eater also enjoys grasshoppers and dragonflies.

Among other birds, such as sparrows and blackbirds, the bee-eater looks very bright and exciting. Even on bird safari in South Africa, you'd still point it out. But now, thanks to climate change, some people are getting a chance to see it much closer to home. Bee-eaters spend winter in northern Africa. In spring, it becomes too hot for them there and they leave for southern Europe, where it's warm enough, but not too warm. Now that northern European summers are becoming warmer too, more bee-eaters are making a beeline for northern countries. As long as they can find enough insects, they're delighted. And so are the local birdwatchers.

In the same areas, there are also birds that are becoming less common. The icterine warbler, for example, likes it a bit cooler. It usually doesn't

ivory gull

great tit

go much farther south than Britain or the Alps. Now that it's getting warmer and warmer there, though, fewer of them are spotted. They're much more comfortable in Scandinavia and Russia. Something similar is happening in North America, with species such as loons, northern cardinals and tufted titmice expanding their territory to the north.

But what about the birds who already live way up in the far north? Where should they go? Planet Earth stops north of the North Pole. And that's a pain for the ivory gull. The whitest seagull in the world likes to hang out around pack ice. They live on fish, shrimp, and polar bears' leftovers. So they're found mainly above the Arctic Ocean and on the edges of Canada, Greenland, and Russia. But the North Pole is warming up. There's less and less pack ice. Scientists have already noticed that the number of ivory gulls is declining rapidly. Unlike the bee-eaters and the icterine warblers, they have nowhere else to go. They're going to have to adapt.

In California's Sierra Nevadas and Coast Range Mountains, many bird species are already doing just that. Rather than moving north, these adaptable avians are nesting 5 to 12 days earlier than they did a hundred years ago. Is it because they prefer to nest when the temperature is just right, or are they hoping the new timing will mean more insects and caterpillars for their chicks? Scientists aren't completely sure yet, but they're going to keep studying to find out.

Not Just the Polar Bear

What does polar bear poop smell like? Just ask Roel and Jesse. Their school organized a field trip to the Norwegian island of Spitsbergen, where students were able to do some research into polar bears. The mission? Find out if polar bears in the west of the island ate different things than polar bears in the east. That would make sense, because there's much less sea ice in the west than in the east. And polar bears absolutely love to hunt for seals on sea ice. Every winter, polar bears have to fatten themselves up by catching lots and lots of tasty seals. But every year they have less time to do this. The sea ice comes later and disappears earlier. This causes problems for polar bears, which is why you often see them looking a bit sorry for themselves on the front of books about climate change.

Roel and Jesse collected poop from the west and the east of Spitsbergen and then took it all apart. They mainly found lots of little seal bones and whiskers. But also moss, grass, and seaweed. And that's strange, because polar bears are dedicated carnivores. If you were to ask them for their top three favorite foods, they'd instantly reply: seal, seal, and seal. But hey, polar bears aren't big talkers.

Roel and Jesse also found a clear difference between the western poops and the eastern poops. The western poops contained far more plant remains. So it seems that polar bears who are less able to hunt seals eat more plants. But you need to eat a lot of moss and seaweed to get your belly as big and round as from eating a seal. So is this diet going to be the polar bear's salvation? That's the question. All the signs certainly say that polar bears are increasingly looking for their food in different places. They steal eggs from nests, eat berries, hunt reindeer, and rummage around the garbage in villages. So if you're putting out the garbage somewhere in the North Pole region, pay careful attention to what's going on around you!

However, you sometimes hear that things are actually going pretty well for the polar bear. That's because there used to be much more polar-bear hunting. Since 1973, this is no longer allowed in many countries. As a result, the polar bear population appears to be growing. But polar bears are hard to count. There are probably somewhere between 20,000 and 30,000 of them. So they're not about to die out. But you can bet that life is going to become harder and harder for the polar bear. Like the ivory gull, they can't escape farther to the north. But their favorite living environment is vanishing beneath their paws—and so is their favorite food.

Nearly all the animals in the North Pole region are having a hard time. The seals live on and under the sea ice, but, like the polar bears, they have less and less of it. The seal pups need holes in the snow to live in, but there's less snow falling. They eat fish, which are moving more and more to the north. The fish eat krill, little shrimp that love to eat plankton. But plankton grows best on the edge of the sea and sea ice. And so there's also less and less of it. Everything is connected to everything else, and the seals are also finding it harder to live in this region. But there's a small chance that climate change will help them out. Because if the polar bear really does become extinct, then you won't hear the seal complaining. Its biggest enemy will be gone and it'll find some way to cope with the other setbacks.

I could go on telling you stories about sad winter animals. Because don't imagine that the walrus, the arctic fox, and the snow goose have it easy. Not to mention the reindeer. There are millions of reindeer. But there are fewer and fewer of them all the time. The reasons for this are connected in a strange way to climate change. Reindeer travel large distances. They cross lots of rivers to do so. The melting ice makes the rivers deeper and wider. So lots of reindeer don't make it to the other side. What's even worse is the freezing rain. In the winter, reindeer eat lichen. They can smell it all the way through the snow. But instead of snow, freezing rain is more frequently falling. As the name suggests, this is rain that freezes as soon as it hits the ground. Melting snow refreezes

too. So an icy layer forms over the moss. The reindeer can't get through it. And if that goes on for a long time, they die with empty, rumbling stomachs.

It really is too bad that things are going so poorly for the reindeer. Because they can actually help to combat climate change. Researchers from a Swedish university discovered that large herds of reindeer could have an effect on the reflection of sunlight. A dark surface absorbs more heat than a light surface—remember? They carried out research in areas where reindeer were nibbling on bushes and found that the stripped bushes did indeed make the areas lighter in color and so less warm than areas without nibbling reindeer. So it would be handy if there were more reindeer—for the polar bear, the seal, and the arctic fox too. And for the yucca.

Yay for the Yucca

You might have one in your yard or in a pot somewhere in your home—a yucca plant. Maybe even a *Yucca brevifolia*. If so, you should take good care of it, because this plant is having a hard time. In the wild, it only grows in the desert in the southwestern United States. In the 19th century, when religious Americans were traveling across the desert in their wagons, they saw the tree for the first time. It reminded them of the prophet Joshua. Not because Joshua had green spikes on his head and hands, but because there's a Bible story about him stretching out his arms. So they called it the Joshua tree. The tree has such a striking appearance that the whole area is now called Joshua Tree National Park. But in a century, there may not be any Joshua trees left here at all.

You see, Joshua trees are good at withstanding heat and drought. Otherwise they wouldn't be in the desert. Give them a big downpour and it'll keep them going for a year. With their outspread branches and leaves, they don't let a drop escape. Under the ground, they also have meters of roots to absorb as much moisture as possible. But the climate is becoming more unpredictable. Drought means that there are more fires. And sometimes there's a very long wait for rain. The water also evaporates faster because temperatures are higher. This is a particular problem for the young trees. They don't yet have the branches and roots they need to make the most of that one downpour. So they don't survive until the next one.

This is bad news for the Joshua trees. But also for the animals in the American desert. The black-tailed jackrabbit and the ground squirrel might be tough desert experts, but if the drought lasts too long, they have to use their survival package. And that's the Joshua tree. By sinking their teeth in its bark, they get just enough moisture to survive. If there are no trees left, these little creatures will disappear too. Foxes, coyotes, and birds of prey will be pretty bummed about that. Because they're crazy about little critters. Without squirrels, hares, and rats, they won't survive. The desert will be dead dull. So again you can see that the survival of one species of tree is of vital importance for lots and lots of animals. Yay for the yucca!

Some predictions say that at the end of the century there will only be 10 percent of these trees left. That doesn't necessarily mean the end. Higher up in the mountains, the trees should manage better. And maybe we can take some of the tree's seeds to the north. That's what the giant sloth once used to do. It ate the seeds, walked a little way, and then pooped them back out. A perfect starter pack for a young Joshua tree. But the giant sloth died out after the ice age.

The Last Golden Toad

What would it be like to stand face-to-face with the last dodo, the last mammoth, the last T. rex? Knowing that when it dies, that animal will never exist again? When those creatures died out, there were no people around. But when the golden toad became extinct, there was someone there to see it happen. Amphibian expert Martha Crump had a front-row seat—and she hated what she saw.

The golden toad was a species of toad that was discovered in the mountains of Costa Rica in 1966. The creature lived there and nowhere else. But there were plenty of them. Almost all year they hid deep in the cloud forest. When the rainy season came, they emerged to mate. Martha Crump saw this for herself on April 15, 1987. She'd struggled up the mountain to the territory of the golden toad. Among the twisting trees, in the mud around a few shallow ponds, there sat hundreds of bright-orange males who were doing their best to woo the females. The party went on for a few days, until the toads disappeared back into the trees, one by one, leaving thousands of eggs behind in the water.

Martha stayed as well. She watched as the ponds dried up and the eggs shriveled. Somehow, the toads knew what was going on too. They reappeared and started all over again. Martha counted as many as 43,000 eggs in 10 different ponds. But within a week, the water had evaporated again. A year later, Martha went back to the same place. After days of looking, she saw one lonely male sitting by a pond. She went on searching for weeks, but there was no sign of any other golden toads. A year later, she went to look again—and again there was no sign of the happy frog gang of 1987. She did see one male sitting there though, in almost the same place as the previous year. Maybe it was even the same golden toad. In any case, it was the last one anyone has ever seen.

You are the one and only

Martha Crump
ecologist

The golden toad made the news as the first creature that was certain to have become extinct because of climate change. Global warming meant that there was less and less cloud in the cloud forest and so the ponds dried out faster. The toads had vulnerable skin, which had always been protected by the cloud. But now that the dry weather was lasting longer and longer and the cloud no longer reached the forest, there were no golden toads left.

A few years later, it was no longer such a certainty that their extinction was the fault of global warming. Scientists came up with other explanations. Maybe El Niño played a role. Maybe it was some kind of disease. Maybe it was some kind of fungus. But then again, maybe all those causes actually had something to do with climate change. You get it? The point is: climate change is hardly ever the only cause of extinction. No matter how loud the newspapers might shout about it.

In 2016, the newspapers also shouted that the first mammal had died out because of climate change. They were talking about the Bramble Cay mosaic-tailed rat. Everyone's heard of them, right? There were a few hundred living on an island the size of six soccer fields. The rising salt water meant that fewer plants were growing there and there was less to eat. Storms were making the island crumble away. Using cameras and their own eyes, scientists searched the entire island. But no more rats were ever found.

To be fair, though, if all of you go sit on a small island or in a forest on a mountain in Costa Rica, you're asking for trouble. If something goes wrong, your species is over. So it's not so surprising that these animals died out. It'll take a while with the polar bears, the elephants, and the sea turtles. But those animals are threatened too. And as you know, if one species dies or goes into a decline, it has consequences for other species.

Up from the South

In some Western European countries, a new kind of ant has suddenly arrived on the scene, digging tunnels under the sidewalk. Creeping into houses to look for food. Taking over the backyard. Pushing out other ants. They protect aphids, which make honeydew, a sticky layer that the ants like to eat, but which suffocates plants and makes cars dirty. And they can give you a nasty bite. They twist and shake their backsides around to spray a toxic substance at their enemies. They're called *Tapinoma nigerrimum*—and they come from around the Mediterranean.

But now they're turning up in northern Europe. They probably hitched a ride with yard plants from the south. If just one fertilized ant queen survives the journey, that can be the beginning of a super-colony. The enemies and diseases that they have in southern Europe don't exist farther north. And thanks to climate change, the ants can also survive northern winters. That's why craters of sand are appearing on more and more streets

in the Netherlands and Belgium, and sidewalks are slowly sinking.

But some kids in Western Europe are more concerned about the wasp spider, which has felt quite at home in northern Europe for some time now. This is one of the biggest European spiders, which used to hang out only around the Mediterranean.

In recent years, though, it's been making steady advances to the north. Although, to be fair, it was already sighted in Belgium a century ago. So even without climate change it would probably have crossed the border. But not so many of them at once. It's recognizable by the black and yellow stripes on its body, which are an attempt to look very dangerous. But it's really not that bad. The wasp spider's bite hardly hurts at all.

What people do want to watch out for, though, is the oak processionary caterpillar. Because of climate change, it's moving more and more toward the north. It can even be found in England and Sweden now. Before the caterpillar turns into a beautiful moth, it goes and sits on an oak tree with all its friends. The caterpillars can be an absolute plague, particularly during warm, dry summers. They eat the trees bare and can be really, really irritating. That's because every caterpillar has almost a million tiny little hairs

that it can fire like arrows, and which are also carried by the wind. These hairs usually just make most people itch, but sometimes they cause inflammation, nausea, and shortness of breath. That can happen even if you don't touch the oak processionary caterpillar and can't see the hairs.

Like the tick, *Tapinoma nigerrimum*, and the wasp spider, the oak processionary caterpillar enjoys the increasing warmth in the north. The caterpillars are originally from southern and eastern Europe. They don't normally develop into a plague there, as they have more natural enemies, such as certain kinds of beetles and birds. Luckily, the great tit likes to eat these itchy caterpillars too. But sometimes harsher measures are needed. In Belgium, they send soldiers with blowtorches to attack the caterpillars. In England, people in airtight suits and gas masks tackle the critters. They have a kind of vacuum cleaner that sucks the caterpillars straight into a hot oven.

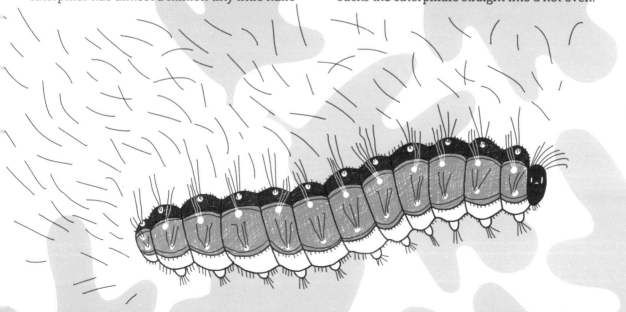

Colorless Coral

You probably have a few shells lying around from some vacation or other. If you're not too attached to them, you can use these for a simple experiment. Pour some vinegar into a glass and add the shells. Top up the vinegar after a day, and then for a few more days. If the experiment works, there won't be much left of the shells. They don't like acid. Because acid dissolves calcium carbonate, which is what shells are made of. And not just shells, but also corals, plankton, and the shells of crabs and lobsters.

Luckily, the oceans aren't made of vinegar. But, as you've already read, they are becoming more acidic because much of the emitted CO_2 is ending up in the sea. Otherwise there would be even more CO_2 in the air. But CO_2 doesn't get up to much good in the oceans either. It dissolves into the water, forming substances including carbonic acid. You know, the stuff that makes bubbles in your soda. Since the Industrial Revolution, seawater has become 30 percent more acidic. You've seen what acid does to calcium carbonate. Poor shells, corals, plankton, crabs, and lobsters. Poor marine life, in fact. Because all life in the seas depends on plankton and other small animals and plants. And, in turn, lots and lots of people are dependent on fish and other sea creatures.

Oceans all over the world are suffering. But you hear most about Australia's Great Barrier Reef. That makes sense, because it's very big and very

beautiful and a very important place for so many animals and plants. But it's also having a very hard time. This is not only because of acidification. When coral organisms die, their calcium carbonate skeletons remain behind on top of the rest of the coral reef. So the reef is actually a huge pile of skeletons. The living coral organisms are on top of the reef. They have a good deal with the algae that grow on them. The algae get CO_2 from the coral and transform that by photosynthesis into food and oxygen for the coral. So everyone's happy. But algae are rather sensitive types. Like the coral, they can't handle acidification very well. And they certainly don't like warm water. If the water warms up by just two degrees the algae becomes poisonous. The coral senses this and says "so long"; basically, it rejects the algae. That's when you realize that the coral's beautiful colors were only there because of the algae. Without algae, the coral looks pretty pale. So it's not a very healthy situation. The coral will keep going without algae for a while. But if the water

doesn't cool down fairly quickly, the algae won't return—and the coral is at risk of dying. Now that the oceans are becoming warmer and warmer, this is a serious danger for the Great Barrier Reef and other coral areas. If this bleaching continues, it's very bad news for divers, snorkelers, fishers, and, above all, for the many millions of animals and plants that live there.

Meanwhile, cephalopods (this includes animals such as the squid and the octopus) are rubbing their tentacles together. All over the world, things are going well for nearly every species of cephalopod. This is no doubt connected to the fact that many of their natural enemies are being fished out of the sea. The cephalopods don't mind that at all. But their good fortune probably also has to do with climate change. Cephalopods can quickly adapt to new circumstances and they're not too fussy about what they eat. So if a coral reef dies off somewhere or a food chain disappears, they're only too happy to hurry over there to fill the gap.

128

•

129

coral organisms
algae
coral (old skeletons)

8 Hydrogen & Insect Burgers

In which you will read... that it could get a lot, lot worse • about the advantages of floating houses • how you can help • how a strawberry makes its mark • why planes sometimes smell like snack bars • why exhaust pipes are becoming a thing of the past.

In short: about measures to tackle climate change.

Okay, So This Is What We Know Now

Since the Industrial Revolution, more and more CO_2 has been released into the air and the temperature has gone up by about one degree. This is super quick when you compare it to earlier changes. This century, the average temperature will rise by another one to five degrees. This will change the climate. Storms will become more severe, showers more intense, heatwaves will last longer. The sea level will rise by 40 to 80 centimeters.

These predictions are from the 2014 IPCC report. In the next assessment report, which is coming out in 2022, the predictions will no doubt be more accurate. There are indications that the sea level in particular could rise faster—up to one or two meters by 2100.

There is also a possibility that global warming has been underestimated. It's like this: Together with the CO_2, all kinds of small particles are pumped into the air, which block the sunlight a bit. If we burn less coal and so on, fewer particles will be released into the air and the sun can warm up the Earth even more. Global warming would then happen even more quickly. Countries that are tackling air pollution are already noticing that difference.

Climate change has consequences for people, animals, and plants. Poor people will suffer those consequences more than rich people. Animals and plants that have difficulty adapting or relocating will suffer more than animals and plants that are more flexible. Because life on our planet is connected by food chains and cycles, all the consequences have other consequences, which also have consequences with their own consequences that … are pretty difficult to predict.

The consequences that we are seeing in the world now are just the beginning. One nasty habit of CO_2 is that it takes hundreds of years to disappear. So today we're dealing not only with the CO_2 that was emitted yesterday, but also in past centuries. Just imagine: all the CO_2 from all the factories that exist now and that have ever existed plus all the cars plus all the power stations plus all the planes plus all the rockets plus all the trips that your grandma's grandma's grandma took on steam trains. And there's more CO_2 being added every day. That means that your children's children will suffer because of the CO_2 we're emitting today. And that's way more than in the days of the steam train. But what can we do about it?

There are two sorts of measures: we can combat the consequences and tackle the causes. Both are expensive and complicated. By combating the consequences, we're preparing for the future. By tackling the causes, we're trying to limit global warming.

1000?
800? 900?
600? 700?
CO_2 : 500?

sea level: +40–200cm
temperature: ±15.5–19.5°C

2100

CO_2 : ± 411

sea level: +25cm
temperature: ±14.5°C

2018

CO_2 : ± 285

sea level: 0
temperature: ±13.5°C

1850

Ready for the Future

From all corners of the globe, architects, engineers, and politicians visit the Netherlands to see how the country deals with water. Half of the Netherlands is below sea level, so the people there know how to keep things dry. Most of these visitors come from large coastal cities such as New York, Jakarta, and Shanghai. They want to know what they can do to protect their inhabitants from storms and flooding. Dutch companies are only too happy to give them tours. They're proud of what they can do and hope to be able to continue their work on the other side of the globe. Many of these tours pass through Rotterdam and the surrounding areas. If you don't ask any tricky questions, you're welcome to come along.

We'll start the tour at the floating houses. Their residents are never troubled by high water. The houses were built just recently and then transported here. A rope attaches them to the shore. When the water rises or falls, the house follows along.

Got my rubber boots on!

Come on, let's go to Benthemplein, a square in Rotterdam's "climate-proof" district. We're in luck: it's been raining hard. In lots of cities, the water has nowhere to go. That's because there's concrete and asphalt everywhere. When the drains flood, the streets fill with water. The sewers simply aren't made for such a lot of water at once. So, during a rainstorm, it's a good idea to hold on to the water for a while and to let it drain into the ground later. That's exactly what they do on Benthemplein. There's a sort of pit there made out of steps. When it's dry, you can skate in it or play basketball or just hang out. When it's raining hard, the water runs off the roofs and the street into the pit. That saves some space in the sewer.

Now let's take the bus to the Eendragtspolder. The visitors all have their faces pushed up against the windows. This is the Dutch polder landscape they've heard so much about. Once everyone's off the bus, we'll walk along the dike.

Wet feet!

"Welcome to five meters below sea level," says the tour guide. Some of the guests give the dikes a worried look. The Dutch don't want to go on endlessly raising and strengthening the dikes. That takes up a lot of space and costs a lot of money. And it doesn't make the river water any lower. When it rains hard, the local river, the Rotte, sometimes overflows. Because of climate change, this is happening more and more often. So the Eendragtspolder has been adapted to collect large amounts of water. In the event of an emergency, the gates open, and the water from the Rotte flows straight into the polder, where it doesn't bother anyone.

Come on, back onto the bus, everyone. Now we're going for a bit of a drive. It's time to tell you something about salinization. Don't fall asleep! Particularly along the coast, farmers are having increasing problems with the salty water in the soil. As long as there's a layer of fresh water on top of it, it's not a problem for the plants. But the heat is making the fresh water evaporate more quickly, and the rising sea level is adding more salt water. Scientists are doing experiments to reduce the salt water and to maintain the level of fresh water. And they're also experimenting with vegetables that can withstand salt water, like sea lavender and samphire (also known as sea beans and sea asparagus).

Suddenly everyone looks left, where you can already see the massive white structure of the Maeslantkering—the largest moving flood defense system in the world. The bus loops around and stops at the parking lot. When you get out, you can really see just how powerful those two white arms are. The guide explains that they're each almost the same height as the Eiffel Tower, but on its side. On either side of the water, there's an arm with a sturdy barrier attached to it. When the water gets really high, the barriers roll across the bottom of the channel to the middle, fill with water, and close off the Nieuwe Waterweg canal, protecting 1.5 million people in and around Rotterdam.

However, the Dutch are already thinking about better solutions. Climate change means that the Maeslantkering will have to close more often. And that means there's a greater chance of mistakes. What if there's a problem? What if the dikes break? So now there's a website where people who live nearby can see how high the chance of flooding is in their neighborhood. They type in their address and read how high the water will come if the dikes break—and what they should do. Trying to escape can be dangerous, as the roads might be jammed and the water could catch up with them. But if they stay at home, they need to be able to take care of themselves for a few days. Wouldn't it be a better idea also to tackle the causes of climate change? And to make sure that fewer greenhouse gases enter the air? But how?

Do It Yourself

Close the door. Turn off the light. Use energy-saving bulbs instead of old-fashioned lightbulbs. Use LED lights instead of energy-saving bulbs. Turn down the heat. Put on a sweater. Close the curtains. Go to bed early. Don't shower for too long. Don't shower too often. Use a water-saving showerhead. Shower with someone else. Don't put too much water in the kettle. Insulate your house. Install double-glazed windows. Get solar panels. Turn off the TV. Unplug the TV. Unplug the PlayStation. Unplug the computer. Don't use a car. Use a bike. Travel by bus. Go by train. Forget the plane. Don't have children. Plant trees. Drink water from the faucet, not from a bottle. Eat seasonal vegetables. Eat seasonal fruit. Eat insect burgers. Eat less meat. Eat fewer ruminants. Don't eat steak that's not local. Don't eat steak, period. Eat less cheese. Eat fewer dairy products. Don't eat any dairy products at all. Use a solar charger. Use rechargeable batteries. Don't buy anything new unless you have to. Don't throw anything away if you can repair it. Dry your washing outside. Use an energy meter. Watch TV together instead of each with your own screen.

Turn down the brightness of your screen. Turn off Bluetooth. Turn off GPS. Make sure the fridge is closed. Use a laptop instead of a desktop computer. Use a tablet instead of a laptop. Print on both sides. Don't print. Borrow books from the library. Only buy sustainable wood. Don't buy chocolate spread that contains palm oil. Don't buy cookies that contain palm oil. Don't buy soap that contains palm oil. Buy second-hand clothes. Give potted plants instead of flowers. Give this book as a present. Separate your trash. Use a broom, not a leaf blower. Don't sit under an outdoor heater. Fill the washing machine. Don't do the washing too hot. Buy efficient appliances. Don't buy more food and drink than you can use. Don't eat fruit and veggies from greenhouses. Don't eat fruit and veggies that come from a long way away. Use green energy. Join Greta Thunberg on her climate strike. Support a political party that takes climate change seriously. Pass it on!

Can you do that, do you think? All of it? Maybe it's a good idea to start small. Choose three things that aren't too complicated but can have a big impact. Eat less meat, for instance. Use a tablet. Shower a bit less often. Once you've done that, then choose another thing to add. But maybe first you'd like to know why you should eat less meat, nothing that comes from far away, and nothing that contains palm oil.

Food for Thought

A gag or cork won't do anything to stop a cow's methane burps—it would just stop them from getting out. And before you know it, that burp-filled cow would be floating off like a hot-air balloon. But let's be fair: the cow's not the only one doing it. Other animals also pump a load of greenhouse gases into the air. Particularly the ruminants, with all their stomachs.

We just need to make sure there are fewer cows in the future. Is that sad? Nope. We don't need to kill any cows for that. We can do it by allowing fewer cows to be born. By eating less meat and cheese. If people eat less beef, farmers will keep fewer cows. So if you want to do something about climate change, then eating less meat is a good start. Especially beef, lamb, and meat from other ruminants. It's better for the climate if you eat chicken or pork. But it's even better to eat insects or vegetarian alternatives. There are a number of reasons for this.

To keep cattle, you need lots of space, energy, and water. That space is not only the meadow or the shed where the cow is standing. They also eat lots of food, which is grown in big fields. Those fields need water. Agricultural machines use fuel to sow the seeds and harvest the crops. You actually need to add in all of that if you want to know how much greenhouse gas a steak generates. You could also use those fields to grow grain for humans instead of for cows. And you can feed way more humans with that grain than with meat from cows.

By being smart when you choose what you buy and eat, you can make sure that fewer greenhouse gases go into the air. But that can be pretty tricky. Try finding chocolate spread without palm oil, for example. And if you do find it, then try spreading it. Palm oil is a gloopy substance that also contains a

This is how many kilos of CO_2 it takes to produce 1 kilo of chicken, eggs, rice, broccoli, beef, cheese, tomato

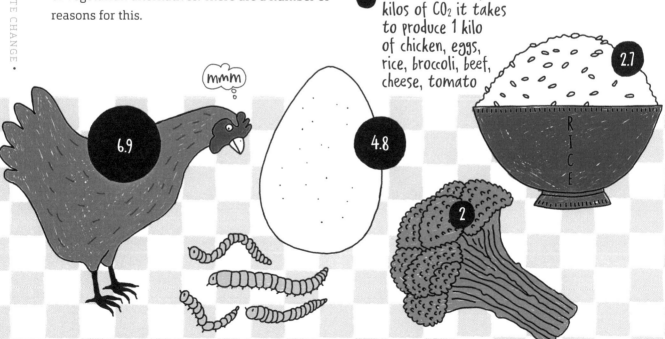

mmm

6.9

4.8

2.7

2

lot of energy. It's used in all kinds of things: chocolate, soap, cookies, chips, cattle feed, diesel…so there's lots of demand for palm oil. As a result, tropical countries such as Indonesia and Malaysia are constantly starting up new palm plantations. That usually means that they have to cut down and burn tropical forests—forests that are full of special animals, rare plants, and CO_2. Lots of plantations are in peat areas, which are packed with CO_2. When the peat burns or is exposed, the CO_2 goes up into the air. These countries have started to make laws to protect the forest better. But is everyone obeying those laws?

Luckily, you can eat strawberries without worrying too much—at least in the summer, when the fruit comes popping out of the ground in many parts of the United States and Canada. But there are also strawberries on the shelves in the winter. Strawberries that have traveled a long, long way, from places that are warmer. Lots of CO_2 has gone up into the air to cultivate and transport them. And there are local strawberries from greenhouses. Which is the better choice? You have 10 seconds to think about it. Tick tick tick tick tick tick tick tick tick tick. What's your answer? The local greenhouses take a lot of energy to heat. So much energy that you might be better off eating strawberries from a long way away, even if they did travel by plane. And strawberries that have come by road could be even better. But it's best to wait until it's summer again, and they start coming up out of the ground near home. Because transportation produces lots of CO_2, whether it's by truck, plane, or boat.

From Frying to Flying

Once upon a time, explorers, pirates, and merchants sailed across the sea without leaving behind a gram of CO_2. After the invention of the steamboat and later the motorboat, the wind did not stop blowing. And some boat makers are now doing their best to emit less CO_2 again. They're conducting tests with ships that have both engines and sails. Some of the sails are almost unrecognizable. They're more the shape of an airplane wing standing upright on deck. That takes up less space than an old-fashioned sail and it works better too. There are even cargo ships that do a kind of kite-surfing. They save energy thanks to a huge kite more than a hundred meters up in the sky that helps to pull the ship along. Inventions like these show that some companies really are trying hard to emit less CO_2. That's a good thing, because more and more boats are coming along every day.

The same's true for air travel. Just take a look at the Flightradar24 website or app. The skies are absolutely full of planes. And it's no wonder: flying is bizarrely cheap. For less than $200, you can fly from New York to Toronto. But the plane would be emitting far more CO_2 than a bus or train traveling the same distance. So making it more expensive to fly would be a smart move against CO_2 emissions. Then people would be less likely to hop on the plane. But governments and airlines are far too happy with all those travelers. And so the prices stay low.

Some airlines, though, are looking for cleaner sources of energy. They're working on electric planes. The problem is that there are no power sockets in the air. So all the energy has to travel with the plane in a battery. The more energy, the heavier the battery. And the heavier the battery, the more energy you need to stay in the air. So batteries will have to become lighter first.

Flying on biofuel seems to be the best solution for now. Old frying fat, for example. If you ever happen to fly from Los Angeles, you might find that the engines smell like a snack bar. There's a local factory that turns frying fat into kerosene for planes. That's great, because the fat comes from plants that absorbed a lot of CO_2 when they were alive. So if you burn it again, it doesn't add anything extra to the air.

frying fat

But planes still swallow huge amounts of fuel. And increasing population and wealth means that the number of flights is constantly increasing. So a number of countries have agreed to compensate for the CO_2 emissions of their planes. They can do this, for example, by planting trees to absorb CO_2 or by donating solar panels to a village. You can do the same thing when you fly somewhere, by the way. For less than 10 dollars, you can arrange to have five trees planted, enough to offset a one-way flight from Vancouver, British Columbia, to Miami, Florida. But of course it's even better to plant a tree and *not* to fly to Miami. Or to plant 10 trees. That'll keep you busy.

Kerosene

electricity

Driving on Electricity

Not that long ago, all telephones were tied to a cord. Do you have any idea how silly it looked? In 20 years' time, children will think cars with exhaust pipes look just as weird. Because cars that run on diesel and gasoline have had their day. Two decades from now, a car with an exhaust pipe will be just as old-fashioned as a telephone with a cord is now. Nearly all the experts agree: electric cars are the future. The only question is whether they'll be powered by batteries or by fuel cells.

The electric cars you see on the roads now are almost all powered by a battery. To charge the battery, you have to attach your car to a charger, just like you do with your phone. Charging takes longer than refueling with gasoline, and a full battery won't take you as far as a full tank of gas. But an electric car doesn't have an exhaust pipe.

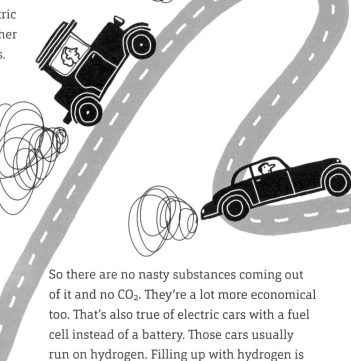

So there are no nasty substances coming out of it and no CO_2. They're a lot more economical too. That's also true of electric cars with a fuel cell instead of a battery. Those cars usually run on hydrogen. Filling up with hydrogen is usually much faster than charging a battery, and a full tank will take you a lot farther. The major disadvantage is that hydrogen takes up a lot of space in your car and at the fuel station. Also, there's hardly anywhere that you can fill up with hydrogen yet. But that will soon change.

Battery or hydrogen: with an electric car, there's no CO_2 coming out of an exhaust pipe. But an electric car has to get its energy from somewhere. To charge a battery, you need electricity. And you can't just scoop hydrogen out of a stream. It's the substance that combines with oxygen to form water. To separate the hydrogen from the oxygen, electricity is also used. That energy comes from a power station. If the power station is burning fossil fuels, then it's not good for the environment. Then the CO_2 isn't coming out of an exhaust pipe, but out of a chimney.

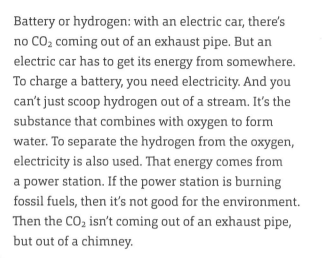

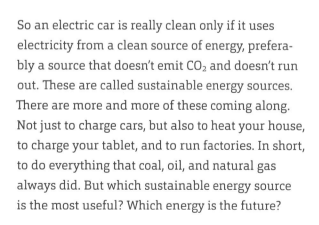

So an electric car is really clean only if it uses electricity from a clean source of energy, preferably a source that doesn't emit CO_2 and doesn't run out. These are called sustainable energy sources. There are more and more of these coming along. Not just to charge cars, but also to heat your house, to charge your tablet, and to run factories. In short, to do everything that coal, oil, and natural gas always did. But which sustainable energy source is the most useful? Which energy is the future?

9 Windmills & Waterpower

In which you will read... how nice I am to fossil fuels • why the sun is so full of itself • why air particles always choose the shortest line • why a million Chinese people had to move house • why power stations want your waste • why Japanese macaques are environmentally conscious • why it's good that prehistoric people didn't build nuclear power stations • what sources of energy have in common with the Smurfs.

In short: about the energy of the future.

NoOo!!!!

Dear Coal,
Natural Gas, and Oil,

You've always been so good to us. There's no way we could have built such a great world without you. Maybe there would have been steam engines run by the power of wood fires, factories running on water power, and cars powered by wind, but it wouldn't have happened as quickly. So thanks for all the wealth and prosperity you've brought us. I also need to thank you personally. Without you, I could never have written this book.

But you've also saddled us with plenty of problems. Just ask the Ili pika. Ask the people of Kiribati. And that's why we want to get rid of you now. No, no, please don't protest. I know some people think you have nothing to do with climate change. But I can give you three more good reasons why you've had your day.

First, fossil fuels will run out within a few centuries. You in particular, Oil. You'll be lucky if you make it into the next century. Of course, there will still be dribs and drabs scattered around the world. But they're too expensive or too difficult to get out of the ground. So aren't there any new fossil fuels being made? Yes, but it happens so slowly. Think about it: it took millions of years to form the fossil fuels that we're now using up in a few centuries. That's why we say that those fuels are not sustainable. But—who knows?—maybe there'll be another ice age one day. Then people will be glad that we've left some fossil fuels behind. They can use them to heat up their homes and their planet.

Second: combined, you lot are responsible for a significant proportion of all the air pollution in the world. When fossil fuels are burned in cars, factories, and power stations, lots of pollutants are released. Sometimes you see them in the form of smog, and sometimes they remain invisible. But they cause lots of health problems. Every year they kill at least five million people throughout the world.

Third: you're not spread fairly throughout the world. One country has lots, while another has little. There's a reason why so many people are interested in the Middle East. There's lots of oil in the ground there. Countries that don't have much oil want to make sure that they can continue to buy oil there, no matter what. And so they stay friendly with countries they actually don't agree with at all. That gives countries such as Saudi Arabia, Kuwait, and Russia a lot of power. If someone annoys them, they simply refuse to sell them another drop of oil. So it's handy to have your own sources of energy. Then no one has that power over you.

So, climate change or not, we have to move away from you, Oil, Gas, and Coal. By using less energy. And different sources of energy. Sources that don't run out. Sources that don't pollute as much. Sources that emit hardly any greenhouse gases, or none at all. There are a lot of them out there. But which one is the best?

This stinks!

Welcome to the fossil club

Candidate 1: Sun

I am the most sustainable source of energy, of course. In one second, I give off as much energy as all of you combined consume in 760,000 years. But yes, the Earth is quite a long way off. So only a little bit of my energy ends up on that crazy planet of yours. Imagine that you could capture all of that energy; if you could, then an hour of it would still be enough to power all seven billion and whatever people's cars, devices, and factories for a year. So I can see why you're building solar power stations everywhere and installing solar panels to convert my light into electricity.

The biggest of those solar power stations is in the United States. No, wait a moment, in China. No, in India. Hang on, how about you go look it up yourself? Every few months, a new solar power station comes along that's even bigger than the last biggest solar power station. And I'm not talking about fields full of solar panels, like you can see in various places in the United States and Canada. No, this is about real power stations where electricity is generated by heating water. You're pretty smart, with your water towers and your hundreds of thousands of mirrors all around.

The mirrors turn automatically to follow me and reflect my light to the tower. The temperature gets so high that steam develops and powers a turbine, just like in a typical power station. Solar panels are another option, of course. That works in a different way. Solar panels are made up of rows of solar cells. The solar cells contain two layers of silicon, a substance that is also in sand. When I shine on the solar cell, a small current runs between the two layers. That's how you can get electricity out of sunlight. It doesn't go entirely smoothly though. Most solar panels convert less than 20 percent of my light into energy. But if you guys keep working away at it, then you'll make new panels that are better and better.

All in all, I'm a fabulous candidate, even if I do say so myself. Okay, CO_2 is released during the manufacture of solar panels and the construction of power stations, but not after that. I'm also not going to run out for the next few billion years. Sure, you're kind of dependent on the weather. When it's cloudy, solar panels don't produce as much electricity. And when it's super sunny you don't know what to do with all that electricity. So you need a battery to store that solar energy for those times when I'm not shining. Not a little battery, but a big one. What's that? Far too expensive and complicated? Hmph, there's always a catch.

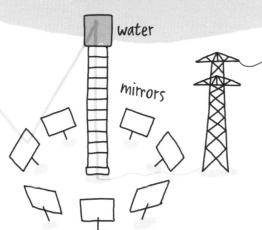

water

mirrors

Candidate 2: Wind

A long, long time ago, people were already using me as a source of energy. Who was it who made sure that explorers could sail all over the world? In the Middle Ages, millers used me to grind grain and to pump water away to create new land. I gave the sails a push to make the mill turn. It's pretty much the same these days. Only the mill is now called a turbine and the sails, or blades, are just a bit bigger. There are actually turbines with 80-meter blades. That's the same size as the wingspan of the largest passenger plane in the world. To get those blades turning, the turbine is 200 meters tall. That is about twice as high as the highest turbine 10 years ago and three times higher than 20 years ago. By the time you read this, there will probably be turbines with even bigger blades that can create even more energy. And no doubt there will be more and bigger windfarms, because people are happy to use me when switching to sustainable energy. I can understand that.

The largest wind turbine in the world makes as much energy with one turn of its blades as you and your family use in one day at home. So that's enough energy for all your telephones, tablets, and screens, but also for the heating, the refrigerator, lights, shower, washing machine, dishwasher, toaster, and the alarm clock on your nightstand. No, there's no need to thank me. Actually, it's the sun you should be thanking, because it's responsible for the differences in temperature that make me blow. Those temperature differences mean that there are more air particles in one place than another. Weather forecasters talk about high-pressure areas, with lots of air particles, and low-pressure areas, with fewer air particles. What do you do when you're in the longest line at the supermarket? You move to the shortest one. That's what the air particles do too. They flow from the high-pressure area to the low-pressure area. And that's what you guys call wind.

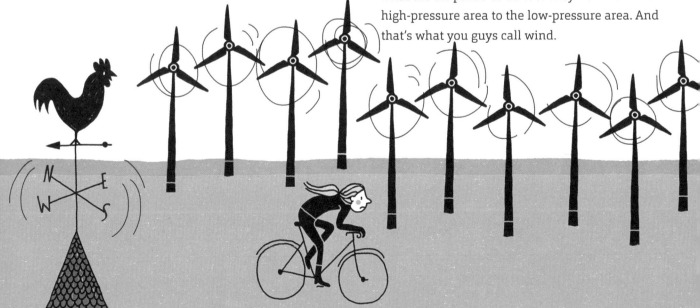

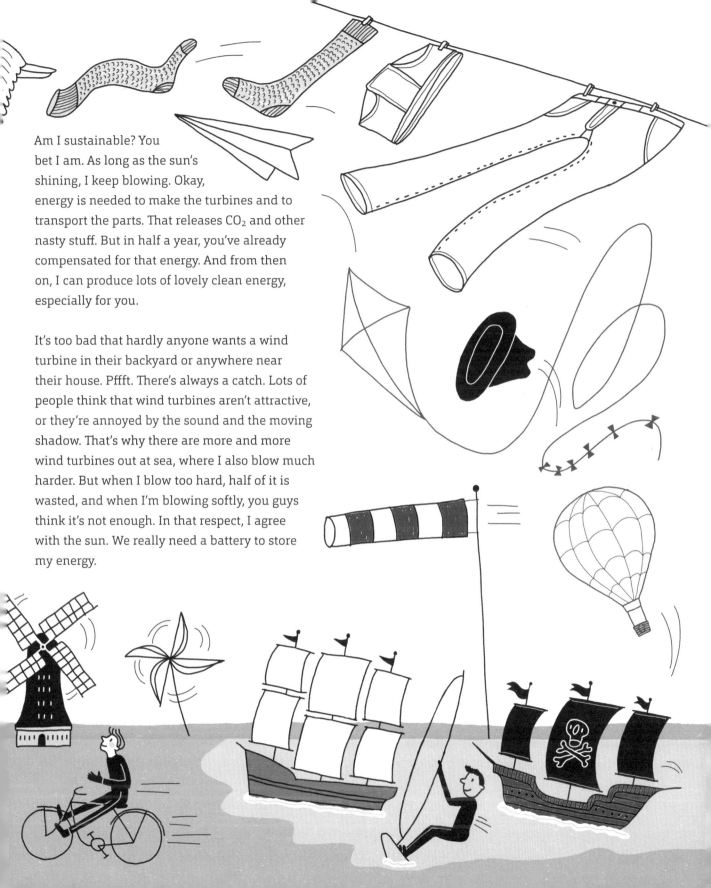

Am I sustainable? You bet I am. As long as the sun's shining, I keep blowing. Okay, energy is needed to make the turbines and to transport the parts. That releases CO_2 and other nasty stuff. But in half a year, you've already compensated for that energy. And from then on, I can produce lots of lovely clean energy, especially for you.

It's too bad that hardly anyone wants a wind turbine in their backyard or anywhere near their house. Pffft. There's always a catch. Lots of people think that wind turbines aren't attractive, or they're annoyed by the sound and the moving shadow. That's why there are more and more wind turbines out at sea, where I also blow much harder. But when I blow too hard, half of it is wasted, and when I'm blowing softly, you guys think it's not enough. In that respect, I agree with the sun. We really need a battery to store my energy.

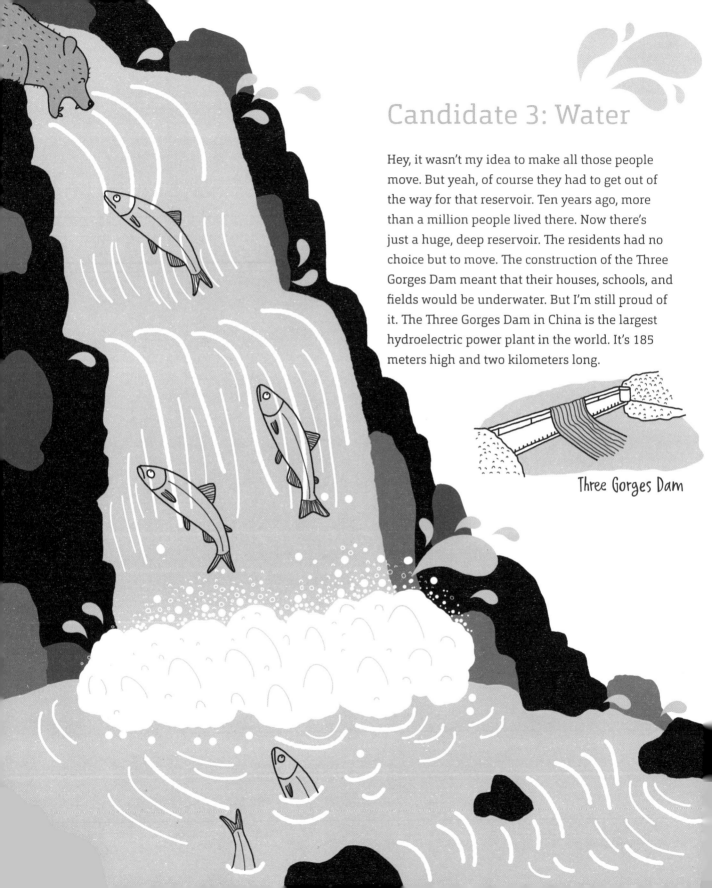

Candidate 3: Water

Hey, it wasn't my idea to make all those people move. But yeah, of course they had to get out of the way for that reservoir. Ten years ago, more than a million people lived there. Now there's just a huge, deep reservoir. The residents had no choice but to move. The construction of the Three Gorges Dam meant that their houses, schools, and fields would be underwater. But I'm still proud of it. The Three Gorges Dam in China is the largest hydroelectric power plant in the world. It's 185 meters high and two kilometers long.

Three Gorges Dam

A hydroelectric power station makes use of my power as I flow from high to low. I'd like to give a shout-out to the sun too, because without the sun I couldn't evaporate and find my way up into the mountains. So I kind of secretly run on solar power as well. But yeah, I do make up the river that they dammed so there could be a reservoir here. Inside the dam, there's a hydroelectric power station with turbines that start turning because I flow through them with great force. The Three Gorges Dam has 32 of these turbines. With just that one power station, I create enough electricity for 60 million people. No coal-fired power station or nuclear power station can compete. The Three Gorges Dam isn't just the biggest hydroelectric power station in the world, but also the biggest power station. There are thousands of other hydroelectric power stations in the world, all of them smaller, but they're all working hard and doing their job.

I'll admit it: lots of energy is needed to construct a hydroelectric power station and lots of CO_2 is released. But once the power station is up and running, I provide clean energy, and you can always count on me. Unlike with sun and wind, you're not dependent on the weather and you can run the turbines whenever you want—at least if the reservoir is full of me. But fine, I know that hydropower also has disadvantages. Just ask the Chinese people whose childhood homes are now at the bottom of the lake. Or the fish who can't swim any farther. Or the farmers whose land isn't getting any more fertile mud from the river. Or the cities downstream that are missing me.

But I have another ace up my sleeve. You can also use me in other ways to generate electricity. I'll give you an example: tidal power stations. These create energy by using the difference in the tides. So that's actually the energy of the sun and the moon, because they make sure that I go up and down in the sea twice a day. Tidal power stations are especially useful in places where there's a big difference between high tide and low tide. When the tide's in, the turbine turns one way; when it's out, it turns the other way. Tidal energy is harmful for the sea creatures in the area though. And if I'm salty, I can damage the turbines. But hey, there's always a catch.

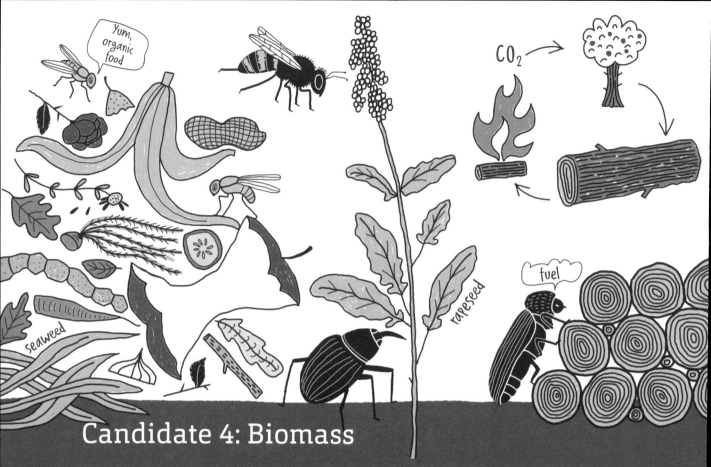

Candidate 4: Biomass

Hi! As you can see, there's a whole bunch of us. I'll just introduce us. I'm wood, this is rapeseed, that's manure, and those guys over there are vegetable, fruit, and backyard waste. Our name is biomass. We're a bit nervous, because we always have to keep explaining why we're sustainable but fossil energy sources aren't. Because people say: look, you're made of plants and animals too and you produce CO_2 as well. That's true, yes. But we took that CO_2 out of the air ourselves, with the help of solar energy. And when we die, only that CO_2 goes back into the air.

That's a lot different from fossil fuels, which haven't taken part in the natural carbon cycle for millions of years and are now pumping their CO_2 into the air. And they're also super concentrated: they're bursting with carbon. All the fossil fuels that you use add extra CO_2 into the atmosphere. You've seen that in Keeling's graph (see page 49).

Plus, those fossil fuels are not replenished. They're not renewable. But in a healthy forest, new trees just keep on growing. So wood is renewable. That's what makes us sustainable sources of energy.

fossil fuels

But, pssst, come closer. I don't want rapeseed to hear this. There are also plants that are cultivated specially to make energy. That's fine with seaweed and algae. But they also do it with sugarcane, rapeseed, and oil palms. And there are some snags attached to that. First, big chunks of rainforest are often destroyed to make room for the plantations. That sends a load of CO_2 into the air. But it's also bad for the people who live there and for the animals and plants that lose another bit of their habitat. Second, farmers in those places can't grow food, and if biomass makes them more money, they don't want to grow food. So less food comes onto the market even though the world population is growing. That makes food more expensive—and who's the first to suffer? Yes, the poorest people.

That's why not everyone is a big fan of us. You should always check out where we come from and what our history is. And don't forget to include our transportation to the power station. That means more fuel and more CO_2. Particularly if we come from a long way off. And wood is only truly sustainable if it comes from a sustainably managed forest. That means that when trees are chopped down new ones are grown in their place, which will be able to absorb as much CO_2 in their lifetime. There aren't enough forests like that. So there's always a catch.

Candidate 5: Geothermal Energy

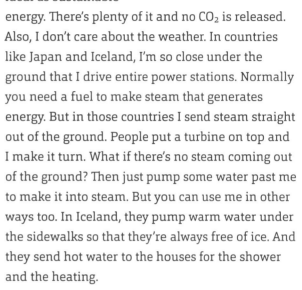

Have you heard of Japanese macaques? They're those woolly monkeys with pink faces that sit in steam baths. They don't just do it for fun, but because they live in an area where there's a thick layer of snow in the winter and the temperature can easily get down to minus 20 degrees Celsius. Without me, no monkey could stick it out.

The water in these lakes is so warm because there are lots of volcanoes in the area. The deeper you go into the earth, the warmer it is. But in volcanic areas, like Japan, I'm just under the surface. Some of the heat I give off is from the time the Earth was born. The rest comes from radioactive decay: atoms naturally changing into different sorts of atoms and radiating heat. Nuclear reactions of that kind are natural processes that have been going on under your feet for billions of years.

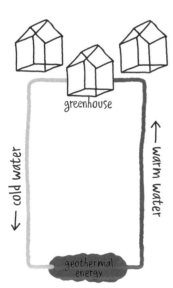

greenhouse

← cold water

↑ warm water

geothermal energy

My heat is, of course, ideal as sustainable energy. There's plenty of it and no CO_2 is released. Also, I don't care about the weather. In countries like Japan and Iceland, I'm so close under the ground that I drive entire power stations. Normally you need a fuel to make steam that generates energy. But in those countries I send steam straight out of the ground. People put a turbine on top and I make it turn. What if there's no steam coming out of the ground? Then just pump some water past me to make it into steam. But you can use me in other ways too. In Iceland, they pump warm water under the sidewalks so that they're always free of ice. And they send hot water to the houses for the shower and the heating.

That's probably not going to happen in most places. But hey, you're doing your best. In lots of countries, I'm deeper down. So you have to drill deeper. That costs money, of course. So deep drilling is only worthwhile for bigger companies. In the Netherlands, for example, vegetable growers have created a heat network that goes down a couple of kilometers. Water runs through the pipes, which I heat up to 85 degrees. The growers can use that warm water to heat their greenhouses in a sustainable way. That's nothing in comparison to Iceland or Japan, of course. But there's always a catch.

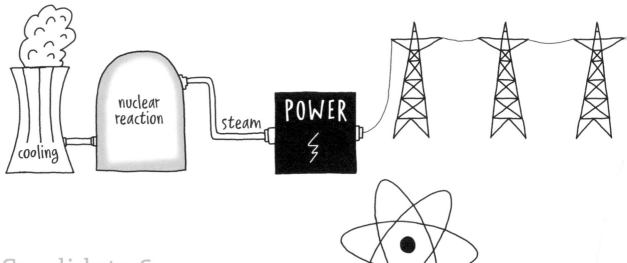

Candidate 6: Nuclear Energy

Let me start by offering my apologies. On March 11, 2011, the worst earthquake in Japanese history took place. It wasn't my fault. But it triggered a tidal wave that caused a disaster in the nuclear power station of Fukushima. Everyone who lived in the area had to leave at once. Since then, there have just been wild boar wandering around. And occasionally people in scary suits who are trying to clean up the land. That's going to take a while.

I'm not involved in many disasters, but when it happens, there are serious consequences. That's because nuclear power stations work with uranium, a radioactive substance that can be found in the ground in many places. Like everything else, uranium is made up of atoms. Atoms are made up of even smaller particles, which I hold together. So you can tell that I'm incredibly strong. Without me, everything around you would completely fall apart. In nuclear power stations, they

split the nucleus, the inside of the atoms, releasing me. My energy makes water boil, and the heat can be converted into movement. And you know the rest.

Why am I the best candidate? I don't depend on water, I hardly release any CO_2, I don't pollute the air, and there's enough uranium for now. Take that! Yes, I also have my weak points. When there's a disaster like the one at Fukushima lots of radiation is released. I really wish that hadn't happened. But did you know that it caused no deaths at all? Okay, the radiation means that people in the area have a higher chance of cancer and other nasty diseases. Which is also awful, of course. The disaster areas will be uninhabitable for decades. And the repairs are costing more than $188 billion. But, you know, there are deaths in coal mines too. And what about the millions of deaths all over the world because of air pollution? That's nothing to do with me.

uranium rock

What did you say? Another disadvantage? Ah, I'd almost forgotten. Yes, I do leave some radioactive waste behind. And yes, the radiation is harmful to humans and animals and will remain so for tens of thousands of years. So if prehistoric people in the Stone Age had had nuclear power stations, then their waste would still be dangerous for us now. This means that we have to store the waste so that it's safe for tens of thousands of years. Even during wars, floods, earthquakes, and meteorite strikes. But hey, there's always a catch.

And the Winner Is…

So, those were the major candidates for the title of "energy source of the future." And the winner is… unclear. There's not one single energy source that fulfils all the requirements. Because what we'd really like, of course, is a source that's not too expensive, doesn't run out, isn't dangerous, doesn't emit greenhouse gases, and is always there for us, no matter what the weather. But as you've seen, there's always a catch.

So there's not one single sort of energy that does it all. We need to combine different sorts, so that they can compensate for one another's weaknesses. It's a bit like the Smurfs: one's smart, one's strong, one's handy—and together they can take on Gargamel. That's one of the reasons why we still need coal and natural gas. You can say a lot about them, but not that they're unreliable. Good weather or bad weather: fossil fuels are there for us. Even when solar power stations and wind turbines are still. Every energy source has its pros and cons.

But developments are happening quickly. Technology is getting better and better. That's why solar power stations are getting bigger and bigger and wind turbines taller and taller. That's why you'll notice solar panels and electric cars popping up all around you. They're getting better and cheaper. So more people buy them and more companies make them. Every company wants to be the best, and so the products just keep on getting better.

If you want a good job when you're older, you'll be better off going into the solar panel business than the oil industry. If you want to be filthy rich, you'd better focus on inventing a super battery. You won't be the only one who's trying to do it though. All over the world, scientists and companies are looking for the best way to store as much energy as possible in as small a battery as possible. So that electric cars will have to recharge a lot less often in the future. So that even planes can become electric. And so that we can store wind and solar energy for later use. Then we can finally say farewell to fossil fuels. But everyone will have to do their bit.

the MOST RELIABLE

the QUIETEST

the OLDEST

the CLEANEST

the CHEAPEST

the MOST INEXHAUSTIBLE

the SAFEST

the STRONGEST

the DIRTIEST

the MOST DANGEROUS

the MOST EXPENSIVE

the MOST EARTHSHAKING

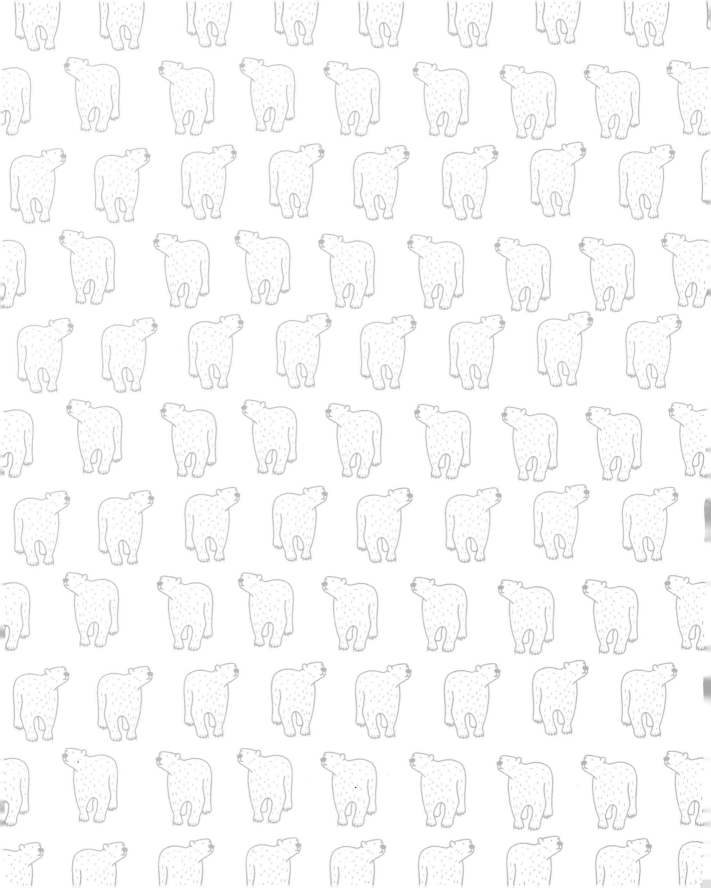

10 Oh Yes, It Is! Oh No, It Isn't!

In which you will read... about a polar bear that never existed • why some people pretend nothing is wrong • how hard it is to make a deal with 195 countries • why statues' faces are disappearing • why we need to wrap up the deserts • who's been a bit silly • why I'm a climate denier too.

In short: about the squabbling about climate change.

Bogus the Bear

Who hasn't seen it? The lonely polar bear floating on an ice floe in the sea. No sign of land or icy expanses for miles around. The photograph is often used to illustrate articles about climate change. To show how quickly the ice is melting. And how badly things are going for the polar bears. The thing is: that polar bear never stood on that ice floe. The photographer cleverly combined them using Photoshop. He even took the sky from another photograph. *Bogus* means "fake" or "imitation." It seems like a good name for this particular bear.

The photographer wanted to make a powerful picture, he said. Which is fine, of course. But the photo appeared in all kinds of newspapers and on all kinds of websites. And now people think that most polar bears are floating around sadly in the Arctic Ocean. Try googling some pictures of "polar bear." Apart from Bogus, you'll find almost entirely pictures of polar bears nicely surrounded by snow and ice. And yes, there is another fake bear. That one looks even sadder than Bogus. It's frantically clinging on to a last piece of ice. That really is too fake for words.

But there's also a real bear on an ice floe. It looks really thin and sad. Is that proof that the North Pole is melting? Maybe the bear is sick or injured. If you find a dead mouse, you don't immediately think all mice are dying out, do you? And one sad polar bear doesn't prove climate change.

But people use these photos to shout: "You see, the climate's changing! The Earth is getting warmer! The poles are melting!" They shout it out loud because they want to convince other people. Because not everyone believes that climate change is real. And if they do believe it, they often think there's nothing that humans can do about it. But what would you do if someone tried to convince you with a fake photograph? You wouldn't believe them at all anymore. Why would you believe someone who lies or really exaggerates?

There's a big game of "Oh yes, it is!" "Oh no, it isn't!" going on. One person says one thing. Another person says something else. And another person doesn't know half of what's going on. That's not the best way to tackle a problem that the whole world's facing. And in the meantime, the amounts of CO_2 in the atmosphere just keep on merrily rising. Oil companies are still searching for new sources of energy. And hundreds of new coal-fired power stations open every year. Because people say: "Climate change? It's no big deal." Or "It's not our fault." Or "It's not the first time." Or "It'll all be okay."

CLICK

It's No Big Deal

97% climate experts
● 3% climate deniers

That's what the climate deniers say. It's a bit of a strange expression, "climate deniers," because they're not denying that the climate exists. They just think that climate change won't be that bad, that it's not because of human activity, or that there's not much we can do about it anyway. You could also call them climate skeptics or even climate optimists. But we'll stick with climate deniers. They say that it's no big deal. Which is strange, because there's an awful lot of evidence that it definitely is a big deal.

Ninety-seven percent of scientists are certain that climate change is real and is caused by humans. That 97 percent includes a lot of scientists who have specialized in the subject. The 3 percent with doubts includes more scientists from other fields than climate science. So the more someone knows about it, the more certain they are. That doesn't mean that scientists know everything. The climate's far too complicated for that. They don't

know, for instance, exactly how sensitive the climate is. How much will the Earth warm up if the amount of CO_2 doubles? One scientist says two degrees, another says four. That's quite a difference. It's the same for the increase in the sea level: will it be one meter, two meters, or seven? So scientists keep on doing research, writing reports, and having endless discussions. That helps them to understand better and better how our climate is changing.

However, you often hear that people don't believe in climate change. As if it's about Santa Claus. In 2006, a movie came out that tried to change that. Actually, it was more like a filmed talk. It was Al Gore giving the talk, a man who had almost become the president of the United States. On a big screen, he showed a picture of the hockey stick from chapter 3. And he went up in a scissor lift to show the highest point of the graph. It was one of the many devices he used to convince people about the dangers of climate change. The movie was a big success. Hundreds of schools took their students to see it or bought stacks of DVDs. Al Gore made a lot of people aware of climate change. But not everyone.

There are still some people who believe that climate change is a myth or that it's all to do with sunspots or something. People like the American scientist Willie Soon. He's published various articles in which he writes that humans have hardly any influence on climate change and it's more about the sun. But he didn't mention that his research was funded by American oil companies. Is it a coincidence? They want to make us believe, of course, that fossil fuels are completely harmless. Otherwise they might as well just pack up their drilling rigs and gas stations.

That's why, in 1989, they started a club of sorts. Around 50 companies from the world of oil, gas, coal, and cars deliberately started sowing doubt about the theory of global warming. They did this by paying scientists like Willie Soon. They helped to generate stories that started journalists doubting. They kept going on about uncertainties in climate science, without mentioning the many things that are certain. And they made a film in which they actually said that CO_2 would put an end to famine, because it was so good for agriculture.

The group had copied these tactics from cigarette manufacturers of the past. They had known for a long time that smoking was unhealthy, but they didn't want smokers to realize that, and they certainly didn't want regulations to come along that would discourage smoking. So they paid people to sow doubt in academic journals and at medical congresses. They shouted that it was not at all certain that smoking was unhealthy. The same way there are climate deniers now who shout that it's not at all certain that climate change is the result of human activity.

In newspapers and on TV, the sowers of doubt get to speak almost as often as the climate scientists. Because journalists like to present two sides of a story. That sometimes makes it seem as if 50 percent have doubts about climate change, instead of 3 percent. As a result, people start thinking that maybe climate change isn't a big deal. That actually suits them just fine. They can go on driving their big cars, turning up the heat, and flying off for vacations. The producers of fossil energy certainly have no objections. They're making good money. Just like cigarette manufacturers go on making money out of coughing smokers, even though they know their products are causing harm.

166

167

The sea level's rising!

1 meter or 2?

It's All Their Fault

That's what rich countries say about India and China—and what India and China say about rich countries. They're both kind of right. In recent years, China has emitted by far the most CO_2 of any country, and India is rapidly moving into second place. It's no wonder, with all the people who live there. "But," say China and India, "over the past 150 years, other countries have emitted far more CO_2, because they started industry much earlier. It's their CO_2 that's causing global warming now."

It's like a bunch of children having a fight. With 190 other children standing around and yelling: "China's right!" "Yeah, but your emissions are way too high as well, Russia!" "Yes, but you shouldn't be chopping down so many trees, Brazil!" "Do something about all those factories first." "But the United Kingdom started it!" These same arguments take place year after year at big climate conferences somewhere in the world.

In 2015, the conference was in Paris. For two weeks, participants from 195 countries had lots and lots of meetings to reach agreements about how to tackle climate change. It was important for as many countries as possible to agree, because CO_2 does not stop at the border. Global warming is a worldwide problem—and one that costs a lot of money to tackle.

How do you spread that fairly across 195 countries? Big countries and small countries. Rich countries and poor countries. Countries with many inhabitants and countries with few inhabitants. Countries that are almost underwater and countries that might even be happy to get a bit warmer. Countries with lots of hydropower and countries with lots of natural gas. Countries with geothermal energy and countries with coal. Countries that sell a lot of cars and countries that sell a lot of wind turbines. Countries that have been pumping CO_2 into the air for centuries and countries that are only just starting. It's no wonder that they didn't really manage to agree at previous conferences in Bali, Copenhagen, and Lima. But in Paris, they did agree.

The countries agreed on a target: in comparison to 1850, the temperature mustn't rise more than two degrees and preferably no more than 1.5 degrees. That's going to be tricky, because we're already at over one degree. And you know from the hockey stick how quickly the temperature is rising. It'll probably only be possible to reach the goal if by

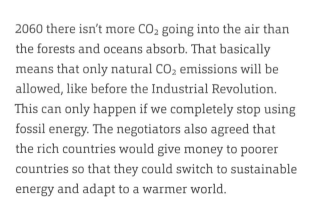

2060 there isn't more CO_2 going into the air than the forests and oceans absorb. That basically means that only natural CO_2 emissions will be allowed, like before the Industrial Revolution. This can only happen if we completely stop using fossil energy. The negotiators also agreed that the rich countries would give money to poorer countries so that they could switch to sustainable energy and adapt to a warmer world.

It was a pretty good deal, you might think, but not everyone was happy. For some people, the agreements didn't go far enough. They're not happy that the countries aren't really obliged to keep to the agreements. And if it works, it'll be centuries before the old CO_2 is out of the air and thousands of years before the temperature has dropped again. Others think we could make better use of the money to adapt to a warmer world. They think that reducing CO_2 emissions is far too expensive and of too little benefit. And that we'd be better off spending the money on good flood defenses, strong dikes, and other ways to prepare for the future. That does mean that the temperature could go up by five degrees this century. It's hard to predict what the consequences will be.

It's Not the First Time

Paul Crutzen
1933–
meteorologist

That's what some of my best friends say, people who are actually pretty smart. "Because the hole in the ozone layer is almost closed now, and you never hear anything about acid rain these days." Maybe you haven't even heard about those problems. The hole in the what? Go ask your parents. When they were younger, those were the environmental problems that worried us almost as much as climate does now. And those problems have almost been solved since then. So why shouldn't the same happen with climate change?

Take acid rain. In the 1980s, photographs of bare forests and dead fish were suddenly popping up everywhere. Even the faces of statues seemed to be slowly disappearing because of acid rain. This happened because sulfur dioxide, ammonia, and other substances dissolved in the clouds and combined with water to form sulfuric acid and nitric acid. And that was what was raining down upon our forests, statues, and lakes. As with climate change, those substances were released into the air because of factories, cars, and cows.

But there were some differences from the climate problem. Acid rain didn't travel all over the world, but fell mainly in areas with lots of industry. The problem was also more visible: everyone could

see that the trees were becoming bare and the fish were floating to the surface. So nearly everyone was convinced that something had to be done. Filters and other solutions were soon introduced to combat acid rain. It won't be so easy with climate change though. For one thing, CO_2 and methane pass straight through particle filters. And also because it's a problem for the whole world. Has there ever been a problem that all of the world's countries have tackled successfully together? Yes!

Yes, really. We can do it. Take a look at the hole in the ozone layer—or what's left of it. The ozone layer is a thin layer of the atmosphere that protects us from the sun's UV rays. In the 1970s, that layer turned out to be getting very thin above the southern part of the Earth. The result: in southern Chile and Australia, people had a much higher chance of skin cancer. But UV rays are also dangerous for life in the sea. So it's a good thing that the Dutch chemist Paul Crutzen realized who the culprits were: the chlorofluorocarbons. Now you can see why they use so many abbreviations

in chemistry. They're known as CFCs. That's all you need to know, except that they used to be in refrigerators and spray cans. Once they're high in the atmosphere, the C comes away from the F and the other C and merrily starts breaking up the ozone layer. And that wasn't good at all.

The hole in the ozone layer became bigger and bigger. But the politicians didn't do anything. Because it wasn't entirely certain that CFCs were the culprits. Besides, the manufacturers of CFCs weren't at all happy about the idea of their products being banned. So they kept shouting everywhere that there was nothing wrong. They called Crutzen's theory: "A myth, piffle, balderdash, complete nonsense." But other people were very worried. The hole could clearly be seen in satellite photographs. Even though it wasn't entirely certain that it would work, it still seemed like a good idea to stop using CFCs.

Imagine you're on a big ship and you're in a real hurry. In the distance, you can see something that looks like an iceberg. But it could be a fog bank, which the ship could easily sail through. If you want

to go around it, you'll need to turn now. What do you do? Do you gamble on it being a fog bank? Of course not. Even if you're not 100 percent certain that a disaster is going to happen, you'll still do everything you can to prevent the disaster. Because if you wait until it's a certainty, then you might be too late. This makes so much sense that it's even in all kinds of laws and treaties.

And so the American government eventually did ban CFCs, even before Crutzen was proved right in 1987. Countries rushed to make agreements about CFCs. In the future, refrigerators, air-conditioning, and spray cans would have to do without them. The CFC manufacturers weren't happy. That change cost them billions. But later it turned out that they were actually much better off and were earning even more than before. And more important: the hole in the ozone layer is slowly closing up. So, my friends, one problem is not the same as another but, when they need to, earth dwellers can sometimes come together to solve their problems in a surprisingly dynamic way.

atmosphere
ozone

Earth

It'll All Be Okay

That's what the inventors of the world say. They think that modern technology can solve global warming or at least reduce it. So what kind of ideas have they come up with?

Let's reflect the sunlight, so that it's less warm on Earth! We'll paint the roads and the roofs white. We'll cover the deserts in white sheeting. We'll put a blanket on the glaciers. We'll shoot a mega-mirror into space and it'll work as a parasol. No, 55,000 sails to reflect the sunlight! Or a swarm of billions of thin discs that will combine to stop the sunlight. Or how about this? Send hundreds

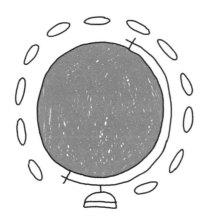

of unmanned ships onto the ocean that constantly evaporate seawater, so that the clouds become thicker and whiter. No, we'll spray dust particles into the atmosphere, to stop the sunlight and diffuse it. That's exactly what happened with major volcanic explosions, and the Earth cooled down a few degrees.

Let's get the CO_2 out of the air. We'll plant forests with lots of trees. Or another even more ingenious idea: we'll scatter iron in the oceans. Not old bicycles or shopping carts, but iron in the form of manure. That'll make the plankton grow nicely, and plankton uses CO_2 for photosynthesis. No, we'll sprinkle ground olivine wherever we can. Olivine is a kind of stone that absorbs CO_2 as it wears down. But grinding it takes a lot of energy.

Do you know what? We'll collect CO_2 from factories and power stations and put it in the ground. In natural gas fields that have been pumped empty, for example. Or we'll store CO_2 in asphalt. As long as the roads are there, the CO_2 won't go into the air.

Some of these ideas might sound crazy, but they've all been through serious academic research. CO_2 storage is already happening in some places. And other ideas could become reality too one day. Even though there are a lot of snags. Most of the ideas would be pretty expensive to implement. It's not always easy to predict what the consequences will be either. And what if in the future the money suddenly runs out and we can no longer reflect the sun, for example? Then it will instantly be a few degrees warmer, particularly if the CO_2 emissions have continued as before. This is perhaps the biggest objection: if we combat global warming using these kinds of tricks, there's less need to tackle climate change properly. But there are already plenty of inventions that might be able to help.

What about the hyperloop? This is a transportation system in which capsules are shot through tubes at high speed. If it proves possible to make the system, planes will no longer be necessary on some routes. That should make a nice difference to CO_2 emissions.

What about cultured meat? Scientists in various laboratories are working really hard on this idea. If they manage to grow meat that tastes just as good as real meat, we'll soon need fewer cows and other animals. And much less methane will go up into the air.

What about the thorium reactor? That's a nuclear power station that doesn't use uranium but—you guessed it—thorium. That gives it nearly all the advantages of a nuclear power station, but far fewer disadvantages. Thorium-based power stations would be much safer and produce less waste, which would also remain dangerous for a much shorter period of time.

And what about nuclear fusion? If only that would work... Scientists have been trying for decades to generate energy in the same way as the sun: by fusing atomic nuclei. If it works, we'll have an almost inexhaustible source of energy that doesn't release any CO_2 or radioactivity. That's why a number of countries are investing millions of dollars in researching nuclear fusion. They already know that they won't succeed any time soon but still they keep on going. So you can imagine how high their hopes for nuclear fusion are.

brilliant!

The Plane Will Fly Anyway

Some people say, "Hey, what's the problem? The plane's going to fly anyway, whether I'm on it or not." But that's not true. It only makes sense for the airline to fly if there are enough paying passengers. So if you choose not to fly a few times, perhaps the plane might not be full enough to make a profit. Then the boss of the airline may think twice about the number of flights between particular destinations. That could make a huge difference in kilometers flown and, as a result, kilos of CO_2 released into the atmosphere. So yes, it is worth bothering about.

The same is true for meat. You can order a hamburger, thinking, "Well, the cow's already dead," but if everyone says that, then more cows will die. If people eat fewer hamburgers, fast-food restaurants will order less meat, butchers will slaughter fewer cows, more cows will stay alive, and farmers will breed fewer cows. That's a difference of 100 kilos of methane per cow per year. That really is worth bothering about.

So you can see that the choices you make about where to go on vacation or what to order at the snack bar really do have an impact. Recently we've been seeing more and more advertisements for green energy, clean cars, and sustainable veggie burgers. That's not because those companies want to be nice. Well, maybe it is a bit. But it's mainly because there's money to be made. They can see all the signs that people want more green, clean, and sustainable products. And so they're starting to make them. The more they sell, the cheaper they can make them. Then they sell even more and have more money to make their products even better. That's how it works with solar panels, electric cars, and vegetarian meat.

Even in politics, it often works in a similar way. People vote for the party that they feel is the best fit for them. Parties want as many votes as possible. So they do things that make people vote for them. Lately, more and more people are wanting something to be done about climate change. So politicians are finally doing something about it. They're closing coal-fired power stations, banning old cars, and saying that they're doing everything they can to hit the Paris goals.

What Difference Does It Make?

That's sometimes what I think as I'm taking a nice hot shower. I come up with all kinds of excuses so that I don't have to leave the shower: We already have green energy. It'd be better if I didn't travel by plane just once for a change. Other people stay in the shower for much longer than me. I just turned down the heat. Factories use way more energy than we do. This book was printed in an environmentally friendly way. Let Shell and Porsche and China do more first.

At moments like that, I'm kind of a climate denier too. I know very well that the temperature's rising, that the glaciers are melting, that the sea level's going up. I also know that we need to change our behavior to make an impact. But the shower's so good, I love long journeys, and I don't always want to eat veggie burgers.

It's easy for me to talk. I live 50 meters above sea level. My house isn't about to fall into the sea.

I don't have any difficulty dealing with temperatures over 26 degrees. My plate won't be empty if the monsoon is late. I'm not that crazy about chocolate and I won't live to see the 22nd century.

But my children might. And your children most likely will. I'm sure they'll want to have a nice life too. Without trouble with food, rising water levels, forest fires, storms, and tropical diseases. For that reason alone, it makes sense to step out of that hot shower. Every minute that you shave off of your shower time helps to combat global warming. Just like every vacation you take closer to home. Every time you put on a sweater instead of turning up the heat. Every day you wait before buying a new phone. Every board game instead of a video game. And every hamburger you don't eat.

But don't start feeling guilty if you leave a light on for once, or eat a sausage roll, or stay in the shower too long. That's no fun, and you won't keep it up if you try to be perfect. You'll soon start thinking: ah, forget about the climate! And that'd be too bad. Because if you take a good look around, we're already doing pretty well. That whole "It is!" "It isn't!" argument is so outdated. There's hardly anyone left who doubts that the rapid warming of the Earth is caused by humans or who thinks that humans shouldn't do something about it. The big change in climate change began long ago. Are you with us?

Put an X through the events as soon as they happen.

⋌ CLIMATE BINGO ⋌

Your first special-occasion dinner without meat	Outdoor heaters banned	First cruise to the North Pole	Flying becomes twice as expensive
Record for highest temperature broken	Shishmaref disappears	First toucan in Texas	First hyperloop route opens
Maximum speed is reduced	Leaf blowers are banned	Sports teams travel by train to away games	White asphalt in cities
First school trip on a hydrogen bus	Your parents get rid of the (second) car	Palm trees in Quebec	Last coal-fired power station closes

⋌ CLIMATE BINGO ⋌

	Gecko in your yard	
Palm trees at the North Pole		

It's hard to say how things will go from here. Every day, there are new studies, new weather records, new initiatives.

And add a few yourself. Give this book extra shelf life!

☀ CLIMATE BINGO ☀

Solar-panel roof tiles	Willie Soon admits he got it wrong	First affordable energy from a nuclear fusion power station	Wind turbines taller than the Eiffel Tower
More than 500 particles of CO_2 per million particles of air	Last pika dies	Ban on palm oil	Los Angeles abandoned because of forest fires
New traffic sign: DON'T STOP WITH ENGINE RUNNING	First coats made from solar-cell textiles	Mega-battery invented for solar and wind energy	More electric cars than gasoline-powered cars
Electric planes	Ski lifts in the Rockies demolished	Ban on long-distance vacations	First seaweed-powered power station

178
•
179

☀ CLIMATE BINGO ☀

Donald Trump gets the difference between weather and climate	First water war	Kilimanjaro glacier melts	Wine-growing in Scandinavia
Record high temperatures hit Siberia	First climate-neutral school opens	Polar bear extinct	Malaria in France
Cultured meat for sale	United States back in the Paris Climate Accord	Cephalopod infestation in the North Sea	Kiribati underwater
Chocolate unaffordable	Formula 1 racing abolished	Hurricane in France	Advertising for air travel prohibited

BINGOOO!

Thank You

When I started to write this book, I knew as much about climate change as the average pika. Well, maybe a little bit more. That's why I'm so grateful for the help I received from people who really do know what they're talking about.

Peter Kuipers Munneke, a climate scientist and meteorologist, checked the text. Coen Klein Douwel kept me on the right track with physics and chemistry. Mark van Heck is a geographer and improved the text in many other areas too. Bernd Andeweg made sure that everything was right from a geological point of view. So thanks to those real experts. Without them, I'd never have dared to have this book published.

On Twitter and by email, I've asked friends, acquaintances, and complete strangers for help. It's fantastic that you can receive such quick and detailed answers to emails with the subject line "Question for a children's book about climate change." Many thanks!

Then there were also the children and parents who were brave enough to proofread the manuscript without the final layout and pictures. Thanks very much to Ilja and Marc Toonen, Rixt, Mads, and Marjolijn Hovius, and to my own Simon, Aniek, and Edith.

Index

Page references to illustrations are in *italic type*.